"The Best Real Estate Deal I Ever Did . . ."

Other books by Mark O. Haroldsen

How to Wake Up the Financial Genius Inside You
Goals, Guts and Greatness
The Courage to Be Rich

"The Best Real Estate Deal I Ever Did . . ."

Mark O. Haroldsen
with Steve Osborne

Opinions and recommendations given herein are based on the authors' experience and on research believed accurate and reliable but not recognized as infallible. It should be stated that the investments mentioned in this book were chosen only to demonstrate a given point or points. The reader must necessarily act at his own risk. No material in this book is given as a recommendation, offer or solicitation for purchase or sale of any security or property. Authors may or may not have an interest in any investment medium or media mentioned herein.

Printed in the United States of America

ISBN 0-932444-03-2

Published and distributed by Financial Freedom Report
2450 Fort Union Blvd.,
Salt Lake City, Utah 84121

This book is dedicated to all those who gave me the ideas and the encouragement to tackle this project. To Steve Osborne for his help in completing the project; Carolyn Tice for her editing, proofreading and determination to meet my press deadline; and Linda Miller whose nimble fingers set all the type inside and out. Thank you!

Contents

FOREWORD

I have a very dear and close friend by the name of Joe Land. (Yes, he's the Joe Land that you've heard lecture or you've read his books or seen his TV show.)

Joe has an absolutely phenomenal philosophy of living that has made his life so sweet and fulfilling; it's powerful, I mean very powerful, and it's so simple most people walk right on by it and don't get it.

I'll tell you what it is in half a shake. But first, let me say that Joe's simple philosophy, that he lives everyday of his life, fits so perfectly into what you'll read about in the following chapters of this book that you'll want to pay close attention. More on that in a minute.

You see, great deals—I mean super deals—are not always super or great at face value.

Most people, including myself, have this crazy notion that a super deal will look just like a super deal when you first see it. I'm here to tell you that most of my so-called super deals or best deals looked totally different at first.

The key to making them great deals was inside me; that is, I changed my paradigm (my way of looking at them) and looked at them from a different perspective.

For example, I recently got a phone call from the general partner who purchased one of my properties several years ago. I had carried back a second mortgage—and the partnership paid me monthly ever since, never missing a payment. But, now they were in a cash flow bind and were saying they were going to have to cut the monthly payment in half until they had the first mortgage paid off which was not for another 4½ years. (The first mortgage payments were very high with a low remaining balance.) My first reaction was one of near panic, since the payment to me was of such size that I had gotten very comfortable and dependent on it. What would I do without that wonderful passive income?

My second reaction was, "What can I do to turn this lemon into lemonade?" Two days later it came to me like the proverbial thunderbolt. Why don't I help them solve their problem first, but in a way that will help me, also. Their problem was obviously a cash flow problem caused by a very large first mortgage payment, but the balance they owed was relatively small. So, why not lend them more money? (I got another partnership with other capital to put up the cash.) So we did the deal with great terms for them and for us.

For them, they had an interest-only loan which kept their payments down to a point that they had no trouble maintaining the payments on the second mortgage to me. And, for us and the partners of the partnership that loaned them the money, we had a great interest rate receivable. In fact it was 18 percent. Everyone was happy. What looked at first to be very bad news turned out to be a super deal for everyone.

Okay, now it's been half a shake, so here's Joe's philosophy that will totally transform your life if you live by it everyday. Here it is:

Joe believes (as I do now; he taught me) that everything, and I mean everything, happens in his life for the best and that God or some supreme force is looking after him with a keen unwavering interest in his welfare and that everything will work to his benefit.

"Are you kidding me?" was my first thought when Joe told me about his outlook on life.

"How naive can you be," I told him. Joe replied, "if someone really believes in this philosophy and it's really a self delusion, so what, as long as the person believes it and it really helps them in their life, like it does me in my life."

And you know, he was right. The more I thought about it, the more I saw how powerful choosing to believe this kind of philosophy was, even if it was self-delusional.

In other words, if we have such a wonderful self-building philosophy, when we're hit with a problem, we figure it out instead of fighting it. For example, you see, if you just choose to accept what you are faced with and say to yourself that it's all going to work out for your best interest, then your mind will be free to entertain thoughts, plans and ideas, and those creative thought patterns will inevitably find a way out of what, at first, looked like a real problem. That's where the best deals in your life will spring from—as you read the following pages, keep that thought firmly fixed in your mind.

And remember to take time to look backwards to some of those deals you do. By looking backwards you will see them even more clearly. Hindsight is twenty-twenty, and with that hindsight you'll realize how smart you really are.

One final thought. Most great deals take time so don't get impatient. Life is spread out for a reason; to live one day at a time, one hour at a time. So don't be in too big a rush. When you slow down a bit and let your brain digest all the facts and facets of a deal you usually can take an average deal and make it into a great deal by building and adding to the original deal. Think, think, think and do it, think creatively with the self-assurance and the total belief that everything you do in the long run will flow to you and be for your best interest. Believe that strongly, even if it's self-delusional and you will see some amazing results!

CHAPTER 1

The "Fixer-Upper" That Created a Lifetime Fortune

If you ask Bill Nickerson to describe the best investment he ever made, there's no question about the response you'll get:

"It was the three dollars I spent to buy a marriage license," he will tell you without a second's hesitation.

Bill, a world-renowned entrepreneur and author who has rightly been called the "grandfather of modern real estate investing," married Lucille over 60 years ago. Today, at the age of 83, he can't think of a moment since taking the vows that he would have traded that marriage license for the most profitable real estate deal ever consummated. Lucille has worked closely with Bill in their investments since their marriage, and asserts that she feels the same way.

A $3 Million Profit

But what about the best *real estate* investment they ever made? The Nickersons don't have to think too long about that question, either.

"There's no question about that," states Bill. "The best buy we ever made was a 100-unit apartment building in downtown Oakland,

California." (We'll call it the Paloma.)

"We paid $550,000 for it in 1967, and we put another $300,000 into it in fix-up work and remodeling. So the total cost was $850,000. In a short time, we increased the value to over $4 million, making a "fixer-upper" profit of over $3 million. That's a profit of ten times the cost of the fix-up expenses, which is well above the minimum profit that I advocate.

"I've always taught that you shouldn't tackle a property unless you can at least double the value of the money you spend to fix it up. People often ask me, 'What's the maximum that you should spend on a project?' In terms of being a yardstick for investment return, the total project value isn't really pertinent. What's important is that the fix-up work you do increases the property's value enough that you're doubling the money you put into improvements."

When the Nickersons (who were then living in Alamo, in the Walnut Creek area east of Oakland) purchased the Paloma, it was condemned by Oakland City Hall. They were going to close it down. Bill found out about the building through a real estate friend. He admits that a lot of investors would have been afraid to get involved in the property because it had been condemned as not fit to live in. Half the units literally had "Condemned" signs on the door.

According to Bill: "I checked with City Hall—the Health Department and the Building Department—and they said that the owner was a "property bleeder" who wouldn't spend a penny to fix it up or make the improvements they recommended. His philosophy was to charge low rents and not do any fix-up work—even if the roof had a hole in it. If the tenants wanted to fix something, fine. But he wouldn't."

The Perfect Kind of Seller

The city was going to close the property down unless something was done. They had been threatening to do so for some time. That's when Bill told them he wanted to buy the property and fix it up. Needless to say, he got plenty of cooperation from the city's officials—especially from the head of the Health Department, who had been a fan of Bill's since reading his book.

The owner was naturally anxious to work with Bill, too, because the city officials were so anxious to close the building down. He was an elderly man, and a stubborn one. He simply wasn't going to fix anything up. "If anything needs to be done, let the tenants do it," was his attitude. Bill claims he was the perfect kind of seller from which to buy a piece of real estate.

The Paloma was listed for $1 million, but after quite a bit of back and forth negotiating, the Nickersons bought it for $550,000, well below the market value—even in the existing condition.

There was a $450,000 existing mortgage on the property (8½ percent interest), which the Nickersons assumed. For the $100,000 down payment, they gave the seller an eight-unit building they owned in Sacramento. And because the Paloma was in a redevelopment area, they were able to arrange a $300,000 rehabilitation loan at 8 percent interest to get all the necessary work done quickly. Working quickly, most of the units were rentable within six months of the purchase.

Recalls Bill: "I asked the city officials to go through the building with me. We checked every unit, and I asked them to give me a written statement of their minimum requirements in order to start renting the apartments. I asked them to do this so that they couldn't come back to me later and want me to do more. Of course, I planned to do more than they asked anyway, but I wanted that assurance."

The building itself was very solid. It was built in 1908, after the 1906 earthquake, so it was built to withstand earthquakes. (In fact, a recent earthquake, which leveled or damaged many other buildings in the area, didn't phase the Paloma.)

A Real Money Maker

Beyond the structure, however, the building was in bad shape. Almost all the units needed painting. There were holes in the plaster walls. The old-fashioned wooden drainboards were falling apart. Cockroaches were all over the property.

"There were 60 apartments which ranged from studios to three-bedroom units," explains Bill, "plus 40 bedroom units which were being rented out like hotel rooms. We immediately eliminated these transient bedroom rentals. City Hall pointed out to us that the 40 bedroom units were practically all big enough to allow us to convert them to separate apartments. That was a hidden bonus that really increased the value."

The bedroom units, which had been renting for $60 a month, began renting for $300 a month after remodeling. From the start, the Paloma produced an excellent positive cash flow. "I was helping to manage it off and on between managers," recalls Lucille. "I could see money all over the place. It was a real money-maker."

The Nickersons still own the building, and needless to say, it produces an even better cash flow than before. The Paloma has increased in value, too. The way real estate values have inflated in that area over the past few decades, it takes little imagination to calculate what the property is worth today, when it was worth over $4 million 23 years ago.

Though the Nickersons have control over the Paloma (their property manager takes care of the normal maintenance tasks), they have placed the property in a trust that will provide scholarship funds for seminary students at Harvard University.

"The Paloma," concludes Bill, "is a good example of the potential profits in fixing up older buildings in downtown areas. A lot of investors shun downtown areas, but that's often where the best buys are."

CHAPTER 2

The $4,860 Toilet Paper Deal

Max Watson—a man who entered the world of real estate investing at about the time he was sliding into his 50s (a time when many people are laying back in their jobs and beginning to fantasize about the joys of retirement)—knows the value of double-ply toilet paper in real estate deals.

He came to this stunning realization back in 1977, when a little old lady who owned a little old house in Loveland, Colorado died, leaving her son to sell it.

The story began one night in a carpet store. Max, a Longmont, Colorado resident, was taking his weekly night shift on the sales floor. One of the people that wandered in that evening happened to be the son of the little old lady who died and left a house to sell. He was looking for some cheap carpet remnants to make the home more saleable.

He found Max reading Mark Haroldsen's **How to Wake Up the Financial Genius Inside You**—a book Max claims he packed around as if it were his life's blood. (At this point, Max was still a novice to real estate investing. In fact, he had only been dabbling in it for four or five months, during which time he had pulled off one real estate deal.)

The Scent of a Bargain

When the customer explained why he needed the carpet, Max asked what he was asking for the home. He said he wanted $22,500. Max

5

smelled a bargain and told the man that maybe he could save his money and not buy the carpet after all.

They met the next day at the house. It was July 13th. Max agreed to pay the $22,500 asking price, which included the appliances and furniture that were left in the home. He gave the seller a $500 check as an earnest money deposit, and agreed to pay another $4,000 at the closing, which was scheduled for August 18th—just over a month away. The balance of $18,000 would be amortized over 25 years at 9 percent interest, with principal and interest payments set at $151. The contract imposed no balloons or pre-payment penalties.

After making these arrangements, the seller had to get back to his home in Cortez. On request, he agreed to leave the keys to the house with Max so that he could clean it up a bit in the interim.

Max took his son, Steve, to the house to help him clean it up. They swept, washed windows, and mowed and raked the lawn.

But that wasn't all they did. "I thought," says Max, "that it was stupid to let the whole month go by without doing anything else. So I put a little classified ad in the paper. It read, 'Just released from estate: older, 3-bedroom home. By owner. Handyman's dream! $27,750. See Sunday, 10 a.m. to 5 p.m.' And I listed the address."

Sunday morning saw Max and his son sitting at a card table in the little house, waiting for a buyer. Max was reading his **Financial Genius** book. Several people came in to browse and carried off odds and ends of furniture and other items that had been left there, giving Max a total of $325 in exchange.

"Looking back," laughs Max, "I realize that I was selling things that didn't yet belong to me because we hadn't closed the sale yet. But I didn't know enough then to realize what I was doing."

Cash and Carry

By about 4:00 p.m., Max was beginning to get a bit discouraged on the sales front. Not one solid sales lead had turned up. "We were getting kind of tired and bored," he recalls, "and were toying with the idea of folding up the card table and leaving, when in walked this character by himself—kind of a swarthy looking fellow who looked like he might just have gotten out of prison.

"He didn't look at the house very closely. He kind of stumbled through it, staying to himself, not asking any questions. After while he walked up to me and asked, "If I give you a $23,000 cash down payment for it, would you carry the rest?'

"I couldn't believe my ears! I was dumbfounded. I mean, this was 1977. People just didn't have $23,000 in their pockets! And besides, it wasn't the way my book said you're supposed to buy property. According to the book, you're supposed to make small down payments and put a lot on contract—not the other way around.

"So I said, 'What was that again?' He repeated the offer. He said that he would pay me $23,000 in cash and give me a first mortgage note for the remaining $4,750. I said, 'Okay, you just bought the house. I'm not sure what to do here (I was new at this, remember), but I'm sure we get together on this.'

"I *did* know enough to realize the seller should put down an earnest money deposit. So I asked him (his name was John) if he had something in his pocket for a deposit. He reached in and brought out two $20 bills. It was then that I realized to my embarrassment that I didn't have a receipt form. In fact, I hadn't even brought a pad of yellow paper with me.

"So I hopped into the bathroom and got some toilet paper. (I brought a roll with me that day.) I wrote him a receipt on *toilet paper!* We shook hands, made an appointment to meet at his attorney's office in about a week on July 23rd, and that was that."

When they met at John's attorney's office, they signed an agreement that simply assigned Max's contract to John (that is, the contract Max had made with the son of the little old lady to buy the home for $22,500).

Max's agreement with John called for a $500 earnest money payment ($40 of which he had already paid), a $22,500 "down payment" in cash (to be held in escrow until the closing between Max and the son of the little old lady), and the remaining $4,750 to be given to Max in the form of a first mortgage contract at 9¼ percent interest, payable in monthly installments of $99.19, with the balance due at the end of five years.

This meant that Max had $825 in cash out of the deal so far (the $500 deposit plus the $325 in cash for the odds and ends he sold during the open house). This was more than the cash he had put into the deal, which included the $500 deposit Max gave to the original seller, plus about $200 in minor fix-up costs and part of John's attorney fees).

At the time of the August 18th closing between Max and the little old lady's son—the original seller—John's $22,500 down payment to Max was released from escrow to pay the original seller the remaining $22,500 of the $23,000 sales price for the home (remember, Max had already given him a $500 deposit). This took the original seller out of the picture. He walked away happy, having sold the home for his asking price of $23,000 cash.

Fantastic Return

Max walked away happy, too. For very little work and effort, he walked away from the closing with a little cash in his pocket, plus a first mortgage note for $4,750. He figures that all in all, his return was $4,860, or in other terms, an *865 percent return on the actual out-of-pocket cash he had invested—all in a mere 33 days.*

"Now, I go back to Mark Haroldsen's book," drawls Max, "and I remember thinking 'This guy is nuts!' when I first read where he claims you can make 100 percent annual investment returns on real estate if you do it right. I just couldn't believe it. But after this deal, where I made close to a *10,000 percent annual return,* I realized that Mark was a lot more conservative than he could have been."

But the story isn't over. Max has a way of pushing deals to their profitable limits. In this case, since he wanted to turn his $4,750 note into the cash he would need to keep buying and selling houses, he took the note down to a local commercial bank and asked if they would buy the "paper."

The bank officer said yes, for a discount, of course. The discount was computed at $507.51. So Max walked away from the bank, completely cashed out of the deal, with $4,242.49 in his pocket.

"Here it was about six months after I'd started my real estate investing career with $1,500," states Max, "and after doing just two little houses, I now had thousands of dollars in the bank in my new Watson Enterprises account—money that wasn't there just a half year ago."

Flipping to Full-Time

By the end of his first year, Max had built his Watson Enterprises account up to about $20,000 in net profits by "flipping" just four houses in his spare time.

He recalls, "I worked awfully hard that year in my regular sales job—I was a good salesman—and I made $20,000, which the government ripped up pretty bad. It really opened my eyes when I realized I had made just as much (actually more after taxes) with very little work or effort by buying and selling a few homes. I had made $40,000 that year! There wasn't a bank president or executive in this town that made that much in '77."

Max quit his job after that first year and went into real estate investing on a full-time basis. To date, he has bought and sold over 100 properties, often making profits far greater than those he made on the little old lady's little old house. But he continues to think of his second investment as his "best," because it fully opened his eyes to an exciting new world of opportunity.

And it also taught him an important lesson. In his own words: "Always buy double-ply toilet paper. The single-ply stuff tends to tear apart when you write up a receipt on it."

CHAPTER 3

Finding the Diamond in the Rough

"**M**y breakthrough property," states real estate investor, author, and educator Wright Thurston, "was a 24-unit property comprised of two 12-unit buildings. It took me from the little leagues to the major leagues."

Up until then (1982), the young IBM executive had invested in nothing larger than two and three-unit buildings. Wright and his little family lived in Alaska at that time, and it was becoming increasingly clear to him that larger multiple-unit property investments were the way to go.

"We realized," he explains, "that because we were living in what was at that time the single most expensive city in the United States—Fairbanks, during the Alaskan Pipeline days—that it made more sense to invest in multi-family units than in single-family homes, or even duplexes and triplexes.

"To give you an idea of how expensive things were, the cost of the average single-family home back then was in the $140,000 range, and a gallon of 2 percent milk cost anywhere from $3.50 to $5.00 a gallon.

"Because of prices that high, it was virtually impossible to invest in a single-family home and then rent it out for enough money to cover the mortgage payments. So I had been looking towards making an investment in a multi-family unit property because I realized that the cost per unit would be less, the competition would be less, my time investment would be less because I could delegate some of the management responsibilities to an on-site manager, I could still cover the expenses even if there were a few vacancies . . . there were all kinds of advantages.''

All the Right Things Wrong

One day, Wright found a classified ad in the newspaper that appeared to be exactly what he'd been looking for. It said that a 24-unit property was for sale for $325,000. The price seemed incredibly low . . . that is, until he went with the real estate agent to see it.

"How bad was the property?" asks Wright. "Have you ever been in a building where you didn't want to bump up against anything because you were afraid you'd get something on you? That's how bad it was!"

Wright returned home discouraged to tell his wife Janett that the property was a major loser. But Janett reminded him of something. "Is it the worst property in a nice area?" she queried.

"Yes," said Wright.

"And does it have all the right things wrong with it?"

"Yes," he answered again.

"Couldn't you use your management skills to turn it around?" she pursued.

"Yes!" said Wright, bounding for the telephone to call the real estate agent.

"Wright," cautioned Janett before her husband reached the phone, "you can buy all the property you want—just don't use any of our money."

"No problem, honey," he called back, dialing the number. "We don't have any, anyway."

A "Don't Want" Seller

As it turned out, the owner was a motivated seller who wasn't involved in the buildings' management, worked out of state, and hadn't put any money back into maintenance and repairs. In fact, he owed back taxes and assessments were due. Consequently, his two buildings were real "don't wanters."

The seller was asking $325,000 with a $40,000 down payment. The remaining $285,000 would be satisfied by Wright's assumption of a first mortgage note to an individual at 8¾ percent interest, and his signing of a second mortgage note to the seller at 12 percent interest, which was less than he could have gotten from a bank at that time.

Wright agreed to the price and terms, but with two modifications. First, he asked if it would be possible to split the down payment, paying $20,000 at the closing and the remaining $20,000 in 30 days. This would give him a chance to get the money he'd need because he knew there would be a proration of rents and security deposits at the closing, which he could put towards the second $20,000 payment. With the closing near the first of the month, he would get more prorated rents.

The seller agreed.

Second, Wright requested that the seller subordinate his interest in the property so he could use the property as collateral to borrow the funds necessary to fix it up.

Again, the seller agreed on the condition that Wright would not borrow more than $60,000 and that he could hold a note for that amount against Wright's home until Wright could show him receipts proving that all the $60,000 had in fact been put back into the property. Wright said okay, and the sales agreement was written up and signed.

The next few days saw an enthusiastic IBM executive pleading with banker after banker to grant him a $40,000 signature loan based on his clean credit record. Finally he found someone who was willing to give him $20,000 on a short-term commercial note.

He went to the closing as planned with his money and found to his delight that he only had to use $12,000 of the $20,000 because of all the prorated rents and security deposits that were credited to him. That left him with $8,000, and meant that he now only had to come up with another $12,000 within 30 days, instead of the full $20,000.

Groveling for Financing

He was in the home stretch on the deal, but the last lap was the toughest. "I wore out the knees of my suit pants groveling in front of every banker in town," he admits. Rejection followed rejection. At one of the last banks left to visit, the banker asked Wright an interesting question: "Why should I lend you the money?"

"I was thinking to myself," recalls Wright, " *'Because you're the only place left to turn to!'*

"The banker said, 'Now Mr. Thurston, do you have a home mortgage with us?' I said, 'No.' He said, 'Do you have a checking or savings account here?' I said, 'No.' He said, 'Have you done any business with our bank in the past two or three years?' And I said, 'No.'

"Then his voice kind of changed and he said, 'Then why, Mr. Thurston, would the loan committee want to make you the loan?'

"I knew I was in trouble, but I looked at him and said, 'If you'll give me the loan, I'll take all the rent monies and deposit them in your bank each and every month. That'll be a minimum of $120,000 over the course of a year.'

"He looked back at me and said, 'I think the Committee will like that.' "

Wright got his loan, pulled off the deal, and spent the next six months fixing up the buildings, using the four-part property improvement program he now teaches throughout the country.

"The bottom line," says Wright, "was that about 18 months after acquiring our first diamond in the rough, I had it reappraised, and whereas I had paid $325,000 for it, an MAI appraiser now valued it at $850,000. *That's a $525,000 increase in a year and a half!"*

Pocket Change

Demonstrating his ability to make a good deal even better, Wright refinanced the property (after separating from it a ¾-acre piece of land to one side of the buildings), paid off the two seller-carried mortgages at a discount and walked away with some spending money that was left over.

How much spending money?

Try *$268,000.*

"And that money was tax-deferred and tax-free to us until such time that we sold the property," adds Wright.

The plot thickens when the ¾-acre parcel of commercial property that was separated from the 24-units is taken into consideration. This lot appraised for $105,000.

Taking a tally at this point, we find that Wright had $268,000 in his pocket, a $105,000 commercial lot free and clear, and still had over a quarter million dollars worth of equity in the 24-unit property.

Add to all that a positive monthly cash flow from the 24 units that at times exceeded $6,000 a month, and you have a real estate diamond of immense proportions.

Not surprisingly, Wright soon took off his IBM suit and became a real estate investor and educator on a full-time basis.

CHAPTER 4

Setting Off the "Chain-Reaction Deal"

Nick Koon's "best" deal was actually a chain reaction of deals that took place in 1969 in Columbus, Ohio, early in his real estate investing career.

"I had just purchased this house— probably about the tenth one I ever bought," Nick explains. "A lady had called me about one of my "Cash for your home!" ads, so I went down and bought the house for $22,000, and turned around and sold it for $39,000. Just after we agreed on the sale, I asked the owner if she would have any objections if I put a "Sold" sign on top of the sign out in front. She said I could put anything out there I wanted to."

Nick got to thinking about the sign. It occurred to him that it offered an additional opportunity. Since Nick was always looking for promising houses to buy, why not use the sign as an advertising medium? Why not put a smaller sign in the bottom panel of the existing sign that echoed his "Cash for your home!" classified ad pitch? Maybe there were other people in the neighborhood that might want to sell their homes. If they saw the sign and talked to their neighbor, they would quickly find out that he was a legitimate buyer who treated people fairly.

The sign went up, and Nick's theory was correct. Within a few days Nick got a call from the owner of a home just two doors down the street. His name was Tom. "Did you buy the house on the end of the street?'' he asked.

"Yes, I bought it,'' said Nick, "but I sold it.''

"Well, do you want to buy another one?''

Trying for a "Double Closing"

It was virtually the same type of home as the house Nick had just bought and sold. Tom, who lived on the same street, had owned it for some time and kept it as a rental. But it was now empty, and Tom was sick of being a landlord. Nick offered $19,000 cash for this one. He figured he could sell it for $39,000.

So he gave Tom a $100 earnest money deposit to hold it for sixty days, at which time they would have the closing, and Nick would have to come up with the $18,900 balance.

Nick's plan was to fix up the house a bit and resell it for the considerably higher price of $39,900. Moreover, he would try to time everything for a *double closing,* which meant that he would schedule the closing to buy the house and the closing to sell the house to take place simultaneously. This way, he wouldn't have to come up with the $18,900 cash balance himself. He would simply use $18,900 of the $39,900 that he would receive from the person buying the home from him to pay Tom. The remaining $21,000 would be his profit, minus the money he would have to put into the fix-up. (He had a commercial line of credit from which he could get the $18,900 in case he didn't sell the home in time, but he didn't want to use it if he didn't have to.)

Sweetening the Pot

All in all, Nick knew he had a good deal going.

But as they were walking out of the house, Tom made it even better. "Are you happy with this deal?'' he queried.

Nick admitted that he was.

"Well, how would you like to buy the house next door?''

"What's wrong with it?'' asked Nick.

"Nothing! It's got new carpet in it and it's been freshly painted. I'll sell it to you for $500 more than what I just sold this one to you for." Tom owned this home, too—another rental property.

Nick looked at the house, told Tom he'd buy it for the $19,500 he was asking (he admits that he would have easily paid $22,000 for it), but he placed one condition on the sale: the sale of Tom's first ($19,500) house would be contingent upon the sale of the second ($19,000) house. In other words, Nick didn't want to stretch his credit line beyond the breaking point. Once he sold the first house, he'd have no problem coming up with the money to purchase the second house.

Tom agreed.

Nick gave him a $1 earnest money deposit for the $19,500 house, and put signs up on the front lawns of both homes.

Tom's second home (the $19,500 home) sold first. In fact, it only took a week from the time the sign went up. The new buyer agreed to a sale price of $39,900. The property was in such good shape that Nick had no clean-up/fix-up costs. In short, it was a quick, easy deal—and a very profitable one. Nick paid Tom's $19,500 sales price out of the $39,900 for which he sold the home, without having to come up with more than $1 of his own (the deposit).

However, Nick was not able to get Tom's $19,000 home sold before the 60-day closing deadline. But he had a buyer who was going to pay $37,000 for the home, and was in the process of getting a mortgage loan on it. Unfortunately, the loan was not scheduled to come in until a couple of weeks after Nick's deadline.

Trying to avoid having to dip into his commercial credit line, Nick offered Tom $100 if he would postpone the closing until the new buyer's loan came through. That was fine with Tom. The loan came in, and Nick paid Tom off with the proceeds from the $37,000 sale. The rest was his.

Let's Add Up the Score

So what's the final score for Nick's chain-reaction best deal? Here's how it adds up:

He purchased the first of the three homes for $22,000, then turned around and sold it for $39,900 after putting about $900 into carrying costs, clean-up costs, carpeting, and paint. According to the calculator, Nick made roughly $17,000 on that house.

He bought the second house for $19,000, sold it for $37,000, and put about $1,000 into it in fix-up and carrying costs. That left him with an approximate $17,000 profit.

The third home cost Nick $19,500. He put nothing into fix-up or carrying costs, and sold it for $39,900 for a $20,400 profit.

Nick's total profit on the three houses in the chain reaction deal was $54,400. And it all happened in a matter of a few months, with very little effort on his part—especially since he hired other people to do all the clean-up/fix-up work.

We will terminate Nick's chain-reaction deal here, although it could theoretically be stretched on for many years. You see, after Nick bought and sold the three houses we've discussed, Tom kept sending sellers to him, with whom Nick consummated at least ten profitable deals.

Friends with Good Properties

Then, six years later, Tom called Nick and sold him his own house—which turned out to be another excellent deal. Some time later, he called Nick and said he was retiring and wanted to sell his business, a small hot dog place called *Tom B's Coneys*. Nick wasn't into selling businesses, but he helped him nevertheless, and got him a good deal.

"I guess he just liked doing business with me," laughs Nick.

"The moral of this story," he concludes, "is that you should always remember that a potential seller can have more than one house to sell, or have friends with good properties to sell.

"Another lesson is that you should use whatever media possible—especially the signs you have up in front of properties—to let people know what you're doing, and what you want.

"And finally," Nick concludes, "remember this: Always be nice, whether you end up buying someone's property or not. Always do everything you can to help. I've had people call me back later—sometimes years later—or refer other people to me just because I was kind and courteous and helpful."

CHAPTER 5

"A Local Builder Made Me Do It!"

Big investors sometimes come in small towns.

That's certainly the case with Valdese, North Carolina's Glen Zimmerman. In this town of about 3,500 people, Glen stands out as a real estate investor who has done so well that at the age of 55 he doesn't even have to get up and go to work if he doesn't want to.

As a matter of fact, he increasingly opts to get up and go pursue his passion: flying radio-controlled airplanes.

A Little Bit Country, a Little Bit Lucky

Glen is the first person to deny any claim to being a *big* investor, however. A "good ol' boy" at heart, he considers himself to be someone who just got a little lucky, someone who was pushed into success. But it goes far beyond that.

Back in 1977, Glen's only real estate investments had been two very modest trailer homes and a $1,000 piece of vacant land. But one day a local builder called to propose something that would shift his investment career into high gear: he wanted to build Glen a four-unit apartment building on his vacant piece of land. Moreover, he told

19

Glen he wouldn't have to come up with any money himself. "I'll show you how to borrow every penny of the money," he said.

"He was just looking out for himself," says Glen, in his down-home Southern drawl, "You see, business was bad and he needed something to do. I was pretty dumb about this stuff. I wasn't sophisticated like some of these people today about how much the rents and mortgage payments and interest and all that good stuff would be. But we talked it over—me and my wife—and we decided to build a six-unit apartment. I don't know why we decided to go for six units. I guess we just wanted to be *big time.*

"So we gave my builder friend the go-ahead. He was a builder, so he knew how to get the plumbing and everything and not have to pay for them until the job was finished."

The six-unit apartment building was finished by February, 1978. Glen went to a local savings and loan and said, "Hey, how about lending me some money for an apartment?"

They asked him to bring in his plans.

Recalls Glen: "I said, 'There ain't no plans, number one. And number two, it's going to be finished next week.' The old boy—he's still up there right now—he said, 'Oh, ---!'

"Back in those days," continues Glen, "they'd send out three or four old men who'd go out for lunch and in the meantime drive by to look at real estate and decide how much they'd lend. When they got over to my property, it was rainy and snowy and muddy, and they didn't want to get out. So I just opened the door so they could sit in the car and look in. They went back to the office and they decided they'd loan me $85,000."

A 100 Percent Loan

It turned out that that was exactly what the building cost. "I didn't influence them, either," promises Glen. "In fact, back then I didn't know you *could* influence them."

Still, it wasn't quite enough. "I also had $1,000 into the land the apartments were built on. For some reason, I thought I needed to get that back. This was before all the real estate investing books and tapes came out. So I went back to the savings and loan and said, 'Hey, would you mind loaning me another thousand, to make it $86,000?'

He said, 'Yeah,' and that's what they loaned me.''

At that point, Glen had no money of his own into the apartment project. The savings and loan had loaned him not only 100 percent of the money needed to pay for the building, but had given him the extra cash to pay himself back for his earlier $1,000 investment in the raw land.

The loan payments turned out to be $801.65 (a 20-year loan at 9½ percent interest). Right off the bat, Glen had them rented out for $185 a month, which gave him a gross monthly rental income of $1,110. Of course he had to pay the $801 mortgage payment out of that, as well as insurance, property taxes, and a few minor maintenance costs. But that left him with close to $200 in positive cash flow each month.

Today, each unit rents for $270, providing Glen with a gross income of $1,620, and a positive cash flow that is more than triple what it was at first. Plus, the original $86,000 value of the property has grown to somewhere in the $135,000 to $150,000 neighborhood. And that's a conservative estimate.

"It ain't no big deal," claims Glen, "but it's been kind of a nice project—especially since it was my first apartment investment."

A Good-Natured Ribbing

Glen gives the local builder credit for having gotten him going in the rental unit business. At the same time, he good-naturedly ribs him about what he charged to build the six-unit building. (It must have been a fair price, since the savings and loan people obviously appraised it for more than the $86,000 they loaned against it.)

"I've always thought he cheated me," laughs Glen. "He was charging me by the hour for his labor, plus 10 percent of the actual labor and material costs. That was fine, but he never did get to work when he said he would, and he was always taking two hours for lunch, and leaving early. But he still turned in 40 hours every week. I could never figure that out.

"But let me tell you, if it hadn't been for him doing what he did, I wouldn't be where I am today."

And where *is* Glen today? In an excellent financial position, to be sure. The positive cash flow on his rental property portfolio in one month is more than most people manage to save in several years. And the time is soon coming when some of his mortgages are going to be paid off.

For instance, in three years he will have completely paid off a mortgage on which he has been making $4,311 monthly payments. That means he'll have an extra $4,311 to put into his pocket each month, above and beyond his current high cash flow.

An Eye-Opening Experience

Although the six-unit apartment building the local builder built was not his biggest money-maker, it is nevertheless his favorite. Why? Because it opened his eyes to the incredible potential of income-property investments.

In addition, it made him more sophisticated. "After that, I really got interested in evaluating investments," states Glen, only half seriously. "What I said from then on was, 'How much is my monthly payment going to be; how much is my rent; and how much is left over in the middle?' And if there was enough left over in the middle, then it was a good deal."

However complex his technique, it has worked. "Somehow in the last twelve to thirteen years, however you want to say it, I really have gotten to be an honest-to-God millionaire," Glen admits. "And I didn't even plan it this way. My builder friend did it to me.

"Not that it makes any difference to me, mind you. Somehow, the money isn't important. But it *is* nice when you can get up in the morning and go fly radio-controlled airplanes whenever you want."

CHAPTER 6

How to Turn a Bakery into Dough

In 1980, young attorney Larry Pino had a problem: he had no money, but needed office space for his firm.

He had decided that he wanted to be located either in downtown Orlando or downtown Winter Park, Florida. One day he was looking at office space that was for lease in Winter Park. It looked good until he asked the owner of the property how much it would cost. "Sorry," said Larry, "I just can't afford that."

The owner, quickly adjusting to the circumstances, told Larry about another property he owned in downtown Orlando. "But you're not going to like it," he said, with refreshing candor. "It's a mess."

And it was. It was a two-story, 1833-vintage building—the third oldest standing building in Orlando. It housed a bakery's retail outlet on the street floor, and was used to house (about 15 years prior) the bakery's baking operations on the top floor. All that was left of the operations on the top floor was a bunch of old, rusty machinery and equipment. The building was 4,000 square feet—2,000 on the top, 2,000 on the bottom.

This property, the owner assured Larry, would be more in line with his financial capabilities.

"The top floor of the building," Larry explains, "had been vacant and unoccupied for years. The ceiling had caved in. The pigeons were roosting there. Parts of it had rotted, including sections of the floor."

23

In short, it was perfect.

Larry arranged a simple lease option for the building. The terms of the agreement called for a one-year option period, at the end of which Larry could exercise the option and purchase the building for $85,000. Until that time, Larry would pay $200 a month for the top floor of the building, and would have the right to do renovation work on it.

Investing Some Sweat Equity

Between that May and the following January, Larry got his hands dirty. "My father and I went in and fixed up the building" he says. "We put a lot of sweat equity into the second floor. We did all the improvements ourselves. I couldn't hire anybody because I couldn't afford to hire anybody, except for a few things that I had to subcontract, like the electrical work and a little of the plumbing.

"But we did everything else ourselves. We stripped the walls down to their original brick. We sanded the floors down to the original 1883 wood. We drywalled. We made it *really* nice. You should see it now. It has been featured in rehab publications.

"I was using my fix-up time and expenses to substantially increase the value of the property so I could borrow all the money I needed to buy it outright."

While doing this, Larry was lining up his financing to exercise the option. He was able to secure a commitment from a bank to give him a loan on the renovated property for 75 percent of the value placed on it by an MAI appraiser.

In January of '81, Larry got the apraisal, It came in at $140,000. That meant he got a loan for $105,000, with a 20-year amortization and a three-year balloon.

Still Mine and Growing

With the $105,000, he purchased the building for $85,000, paid himself back for all that he had put into rehabilitating the building, and had about $12,000 left over to put into his pocket. Plus, he had a free home for his offices on the top floor while he continued to rent out the bottom floor.

"I've owned the building ever since," he adds.

And he has put it to good use. In 1984, Larry bought a similar building right next to it, knocked out some walls in between, and combined the two. Today, his own offices are housed in the 4,000 square feet on the top floor of the combined buildings, and he leases out the ground floor's 4,000 square feet to two restaurants for a total rent of $4,400 per month.

The last appraisal Larry ordered on the property—three years ago—came in at $725,000. He points out that if you worked out the current value on a normal capitalization rate basis, it would be worth about $850,000 today.

The renovated bakery has also been a source of capital. Larry explains: "As it went up in value, I have borrowed money against it to invest in other buildings. Actually, I've borrowed $540,000 against the property at different times over a ten-year period. And even with borrowing against it, and with using the entire top floor for my own operations, it continues to produce a nice positive cash flow."

Larry's bakery building deal produced benefits beyond mere financial ones. He claims that it taught him the value of lease options as a tool to help people with little money to create wealth in real estate. Another lesson it taught him is that you can often substantially increase a property's value by altering its use. By converting a manufacturing/retail facility to a retail/office building, he reaped a stunning investment return.

"That's why I say it was the best of my investments by far," he concludes.

CHAPTER 7

Two for Less Than the Price of One

When Cincinnati entrepreneur Harry Leyman launched his real estate investing career in 1980, he went into it as a business—not as a hobby, sideline , or retirement fund. In fact, he abhors the word "investor" because, as he says, "Every time I've bought a building, I've bought myself a *job.*" In other words, real estate is a hands-on proposition for this investor, who also happens to be a founder and past president of the Real Estate Investors Association of Cincinnati.

Just Across the River

Harry's best deal came along about five or six years into his career. "I was doing a rehab," he recalls, "having a roof and a deck put on a house that I bought, and I told the subcontractor to give me a call if he knew of any houses that were available.

"About three weeks later, he called. 'I know a lady over here in Covington, Kentucky, (across the river from Cincinnati)' he said. 'Her brother died and left her two houses. She just wants to get rid of them. She'll take $24,000 for both of them.' "

One was a three-bedroom house. The other was a two-bedroom

cottage, often called a "shotgun house" in the South. With a sales price of $24,000, Harry's first question was to ask if they were inhabitable. The subcontractor assured him they were. In fact, he pointed out, one currently was rented, and the other was the one the man was living in when he died.

"I went over to look at them with the sister of the deceased," says Harry, "and it was true. She wanted $24,000 for *both houses.* I didn't even neogtiate with her. I wrote up a contract for $24,000 cash with a 60-day closing."

Harry immediately went to work to sell the properties. He sold the three-bedroom home within a short time for $29,900. After paying the $24,000 contract price to the seller, he had $5,900 left over. Plus, he still had a two-bedroom cottage left to sell, which he now owned free and clear.

Remember, Harry had put none of his own money into this deal, and he didn't have to do anything or make any improvements to either of the homes. After just a week or two, he now had $5,900 in his pocket *plus* a two-bedroom cottage that was completely paid off. "The way I looked at it," he quips, "it's like I was paid $5,900 to take that second property."

A Deal She Couldn't Refuse

Harry's next move was to sell the cottage. He did this very easily by making the tenant who already lived in it a deal she couldn't refuse. She had been paying $200 a month for rent. Harry let her buy it for $20,000, payable in $200 monthly mortgage payments for 30 years, with *no down payment.* He carried the full $20,000 contract.

Says Harry, "Now, that's 360 months. If you multiply 360 months by $200, you get $72,000. That's what I got for that little cottage—what I'm still getting, I should say.

"If you add that to the $5,900 I had left over after selling the three-bedroom home and paying off both houses, I think that's a pretty sweet deal. And it was a sweet deal for the lady who bought the cottage, too. She didn't have to come up with a dime to buy the house. She just went on making her $200 payments, only now it was to *buy* the home, not to rent it. And she didn't have to worry about rent increases."

There are some lessons to be learned from Harry's best deal:

1. *You never know where you're going to find good deals, so you've got to ask everybody.* In other words, get the word out and keep it circulating.

2. *He who gives the price first, loses.* If Harry had made an offer for the two houses before the lady told him the price, he would have offered more, simply because $24,000 for the two properties was lower than he would have thought she would ever have accepted.

3. *If you want to buy properties for nothing down, you should consider selling them for nothing down.* Harry explains that in the case of the two-bedroom cottage, this strategy turned out to be safe because the tenant already had a good track record of making rent payments of the same amount. "And because I didn't have any money in it, it sure made sense for me to sell it to her for nothing down. The way I see it, 'what goes around comes around.' If I can help someone own a house, it makes me feel real good."

Turning $24,000 into $76,900 makes Harry feel good, too. "That's the beauty of real estate," he claims. "If you do it right and go about it with the right attitude, you can do deals that will make everyone a winner."

Golden Returns in Golden Valley

U nlike many real estate entrepreneurs, Doug Marr has ventured beyond his own geographical market (he lives in Upland, California) and has done very well on "foreign" turf.

Doug, who has been investing in earnest since 1974, began making trips with his brother in about 1987 to scout out an area that showed promises of being "hot."

"We went to Laughlin, Nevada," he explained, "and right across the Colorado River to Bullhead City, Arizona. (The two cities are like one population center split by a river.) Laughlin is where they've been building a lot of new casinos. In fact, it's now the third largest gambling city in Nevada. It's been growing rapidly in the last few years with quite a few big new casinos opening."

A Real "Golden" Valley

There is an approximate 30-mile drive from Bullhead City to the town of Kingman, Arizona. Midway between these two cities is an area called Golden Valley. It is on the main route coming from the east going to the gambling area. Consequently, a lot of traffic flows through it. Fortunately, although Golden Valley is basically a desert,

29

plenty of water lies underground waiting to be brought up through wells.

"We went out there," recalls Doug, "and realized that there would definitely be a lot of growth in that area, with the casinos and all the employees that would be coming in. Also, there are a lot of "snowbirds" that would descend on the area in the winter. You could see the property values going up."

Doug and his brother bought a couple of townhouse lots each in a new section of Bullhead, and built on them. As they did this, they naturally began nosing around the area. They kept hearing about a place called Golden Valley. Originally, they decided to buy a couple of two- to four-acre parcels there for $2,000 to $4,000 each, and hold them for their kids.

One day in 1988, a Realtor was driving Doug around the area, and said, "There's a 40-acre parcel over here that has an old mobile home on it. He's asking $42,000 for everything."

Recalls Doug, "I figured I could haul the mobile home off and get rid of it, and keep the 40 acres for the future. So instead of buying a 2½-acre parcel, I had some money available, so I paid cash for the 40 acres and trailer. Before I closed escrow, I went over and looked at the mobile home. I was surprised. It wasn't that bad. It had been leased out and was a complete mess, with diapers all over. But I realized I could clean it, fix it up and rent it out."

He did. Unfortunately, the location was so remote that he found it. impossible to keep things in and on the mobile home from being stolen. "So my brother and I bought a 2½-acre parcel in an area that wasn't so remote," he explains. "We split it and I had the trailer hauled over and installed on my 1¼-acre piece. I put about $18,000 into the land, moving and installing the trailer home, and all that. Now I have the trailer home rented out for $425 a month. So I'm getting a good return from that."

A Sideline for the Best

All of this was nothing more than a sideline to Doug's best deal, however. The *real* deal revolved around the 40 acres of raw land.

"When I bought it," remarks Doug, "there was talk of drilling wells and putting water lines in to the area. They're in the process of doing that right now, and the first area to have trunk lines in goes to my property—on two sides of it.

"They were also in the process of getting funds from the state to widen the highway, which they're now in the process of doing. And they're building an airport expansion in Bullhead City that will soon accommodate 737s and bring in flights from all over the country.

"Plus, they're soon going to be paving the roads from the highway, which have just been dirt up to this point. In fact, they're paving a road that happens to go right by my property.

"All these things have added to the growth in the area, and have increased interest in the valley *and* property values. A few projects have already gone through county planning approvals and are just waiting for the water to go in to start building. Of course, they've levied an assessment for all this, but it's only about $8,000 for my whole parcel. And I can pay that off over a ten-year period."

Filling Up Fast

Because of all the casino employees coming into the area, the lack of housing, and these improvements, the Golden Valley area is quickly becoming a prime location.

"Golden Valley property similar to mine that you could have bought not too long ago for $1,000 an acre has skyrocketed," Doug attests. "They're suggesting I put my parcel on the market now for $15,000 per acre. The parcel next to mine recently had an offer for $12,500 per acre, but it has a wash going through it, and mine doesn't. At $15,000 an acre for my 40 acres, you're talking about $600,000 for a $42,000 investment. (Actually, less than $42,000 because it no longer includes the mobile home.) That's a *1,500 percent gain* in just over two years!"

Like so many investors, Doug would rather not leave any of his own money tied up in a project. After all, cash is the lifeblood of high-value investments. So he contacted his brother, a pilot for Delta Airlines, and told him that he'd give him a first trust deed on the 40-acre parcel if he wanted to loan him some money. His brother agreed and gave Doug $50,000 at 12 percent interest (interest-only payments of $500 a month).

This repaid Doug for the $42,000 he paid for the land, and gave him several thousand dollars to put in his pocket.

Golden Valley Gold Mine

Doug has learned an important lesson from his Golden Valley project: get out and do the footwork. He says that after he did his homework, talked to the area's Realtors and government officials, poured over topographic maps, walked the land, and studied the values and demographics in the area, he got to the point where he knew more than the Realtors did.

"I will probably sell the parcel this year," claims Doug. "I'm waiting to list it until we've got the water in the ground and the paving started. But I've already told the Realtors in the area that I will sell it now for $600,000 if they have a buyer. When the improvements are complete, it should be worth more than that.

"It's a viable property," Doug concludes, "and it has been very good for me."

It doesn't take a calculator to realize that that's an understatement.

CHAPTER 9

Doin' The Texas "Quick Flip"

Patti Clampitt proves that little investors and little properties can turn big profits.

In fact, this Fort Worth real estate entrepreneur has proven time and time again since she launched her career in 1985 that she could "flip" low-end houses to create high-end profits.

Back in 1987, Patti received a call from an acquaintance of hers that worked at a mortgage company. Her friend told her about a single-family home in nearby Burleson that the company had had to take back. It was appraised at $77,000, but they'd take substantially less to get it off their books by a certain date. "You'd better get out to this house fast," she said, "because a lot of other investors are going to be hot on this property."

Patti asked what would be the very lowest price the mortgage company would accept. Her friend, working with a formula, told her that that price would be $48,780, but pointed out that they would try to get a lot more than that. In fact, they were asking $69,000 at that time.

The house was a brick, three-bedroom, two bathroom, two-car garage home of about 1,600 square feet. It was located in a nice neighborhood. Says Patti: "I knew the minute I saw it that it was going to be a good investment. This house, retail, should have been at least $75,000. And it was in a nice, nice area."

Negotiating with the Bank

Patti decided to make an all cash offer of $44,000. She made it lower than the minimum she knew they could accept in order to give herself some room to negotiate. They came back with $58,000. She moved up a little.

The closer the mortgage company came to its deadline, the more they lowered the price. During negotiations, Patti stressed the fact that she was making a cash offer, which meant that they should be able to reduce the price much more than they could for an offer that they'd have to turn around and finance.

In mid-January, with the deadline fast approaching, they settled on a cash purchase price of $48,780. (Her friend's calculations had been right.) Patti gave the mortgage company an earnest money deposit of $500. and the closing date was set for a week later, on January 23, at which time Patti would deliver the $48,280 balance and take title to the house.

"I put a 'For Sale' sign in the window as soon as we signed the agreement," recalls Patti. "As it happened, the lady who lived just across the street called me as soon as she saw the sign. She had a mother that wanted to move into the neighborhood.

"The daughter was kind of ticked off, because they had called the mortgage company to try to buy the house about six months prior to this when she found out they had foreclosed on it. They had made a cash offer of $69,000 to buy the home, but the mortgage company refused it.

"So I said I'd sell it to them for $68,900, and the daughter was tickled pink. But she was also a little confused. She said, 'I don't know how in the world you bought it for less, because they wouldn't even talk to me.' I knew it was because the mortgage company had softened a lot since that time, but I didn't say too much."

A Week's Worth of Profit

Patti's plan was to go ahead with the closing to buy the home from the mortgage company on the 23rd, and then have a closing to sell the home to the new buyer 30 minutes later.

"The lady said they were going to pay cash," recalls Patti. "I was skeptical. You always hear people say, 'I'll just pay cash,' and I always say, 'Oh, sure.' So really, I was worried about this deal going through at all."

But it did. Everything went as planned. Patti bought the home on January 23 from the mortgage company for a total cash price of $48,780. Then, 30 minutes later, she turned around and sold it to the mother of the lady across the street for $68,900 cash. The difference, for those without calculators at hand, is $20,120.

The life span of the entire deal was about a week. All Patti did during that time—other than negotiate and sign papers—was to install an exhaust hood over the stove and make a few other minor repairs, which cost a total of $112 and a couple of hours of her time.

Patti also had closing costs, of course. Buying the home cost her $115 in closing costs and selling it cost $648 (mostly for title insurance). Deducting those costs and the $112 repair expenses from the $20,120 gross profit, she realized a net profit of $19,245.

A *$19,245 profit for a few hours work* on a small, single-family home . . . with deals like that, little Patti Clampitt qualifies as a big investor in anyone's book.

CHAPTER 10

A Great Deal . . . from Beginning to End

" **Y**ou never know how good a deal is until you sell it," states Bill Neuman, a real estate entrepreneur from St. Charles, Illinois. "When you pick up the chips at the end of the card game, that's when you know who won."

Bill's favorite real estate deal—his second—spanned a decade and left a lot of chips on the table. "I've seen it through to the very end, and I know it was a good deal because it's now a done deal," he adds. "In contrast, I have a property right now that I've made about a half million dollars on in the past couple of years, but I haven't sold it yet, so I don't really know how good an investment it's going to be."

Bill got into his second real estate deal back in October of 1980, after making a mediocre to poor showing with his first investment. "After the first one, I started subscribing to the **Financial Freedom Report**," he recalls. "That was literally my salvation. I learned about creative financing, property value analysis, discount property value analysis, discounting sellers' notes—basically how to do it right."

Cash at Closing

In October, 1980, Bill found a two-year-old fourplex apartment property through a real estate agent. It was located right on the bank of the Fox River in neighboring Geneva, across from a park. It was in excellent condition. All the units were occupied with solid tenants.

The property had appraised for $156,000, and Bill purchased it at near market value for $154,000. He assumed an existing $118,000 first mortgage at about 9½ percent interest. The seller took back a $26,000 second mortgage, with interest-only payments for three years, at which time it would become due and payable.

That left a down payment of $10,000 which Bill secured in the form of an interest-only personal loan from his father.

"When we closed," says Bill, "because of the prorations of taxes, security deposits, and rents, I took about $2,000 cash away with me. So I purchased the whole thing with none of my own cash, and walked away from the closing table with about $2,000.

Just before the closing, Bill read an article about discounting sellers' notes. He admits that he had to read the article twice because he didn't even know it could be done. So at the closing, he offered to pay off the seller's $26,000 note at a discounted price. The seller refused the offer.

That was in October of '80. The following February, just four months later, the seller called Bill and asked if his offer was still good. He was going through a divorce and a business bankruptcy simultaneously, and he needed cash fast. Bill offered him $17,000 for the $26,000 note, and they finally settled on $20,000, which gave Bill a $6,000 discount.

Bill got the $20,000 pay-off amount from a bank, and ended up paying less per month for the three-year, interest-only bank mortgage loan than he had been paying to the seller.

A Winner in the Making

Bill's new property turned out to be a winner. In the first year, he had a break-even cash flow, which turned into a positive cash flow in all subsequent years. "The last year I owned it," he says, "it was giving me an approximate $7,000 positive cash flow after all expenses and debt service."

The rents were $325 per month per unit when Bill first purchased the property, so he promptly raised them to $350. He admits that he was afraid that half the tenants would move.

But no one did. By the time Bill sold the property, the rents were $645. (He gave one tenant—the on-site manager—a $30 rent discount, however. Because of this, plus the fact that the property was relatively new and well maintained, Bill rarely had to do anything in terms of physical maintenance.)

"During the entire time I owned the fourplex, I had only a half-month vacancy in one unit," Bill points out, "and that's only because an elderly tenant passed away, obviously without giving notice. It was amazing. In fact, we had very low turnover while I owned it. There was even a three-year period during which *not one tenant moved.*"

Because the fourplex was appreciating in value 6 to 7 percent a year, Bill decided it was time to refinance and take some cash out about five years after he bought it. So in 1985, he refinanced with a $175,000 first mortgage, which still allowed him a healthy positive cash flow.

With the $175,000, he paid off the original first mortgage (which had been paid down to about $115,000 from $118,000). This left him with $60,000 cash. With that, he paid off the second mortgage— the $20,000 interest-only bank loan which he had extended for a few years after the original three-year term—and still had $40,000 left over to line his pockets.

"I used this $40,000 to finance other real estate investments," Bill asserts. "When I refinance properties, I never *ever* use the cash I take out for personal things. It is always used to leverage more property investments."

I Loved This Property

The $10,000 personal loan he received from his father in the beginning is still in force. Bill continues to pay him $1,000 a year interest, but doesn't plan to pay off the balance for two reasons. First, his father would rather go on getting the $1,000 a year interest; and second, his sister borrowed an equal amount, and they all decided it would be best to settle out of the father's estate, when that time comes.

"In 1990," explains Bill, "I wasn't going to sell this property. I loved it. It was turning a nice cash flow. It was appreciating. It stayed full. And it didn't take much work at all. You could argue that ten years is a little too long to own the property because of depreciation. When I bought it, I got double declining balance depreciation, so my depreciation was no longer very attractive.

"But a real estate broker I know came to me and said he'd like to present a buyer for my building. I told him it wasn't for sale. He said, 'Name your price.' I said, 'Brad, any price that I'd name would be too high because I'm not a motivated seller—believe me.'

"He was very persistent in a very professional way, so I finally said, 'Okay, I'll name a price, but I don't want a bunch of tire-kickers looking at my property and bothering my tenants. If you want to send me one buyer who will meet my price, fine. But I don't want any hassle here.' "

Bill's price was $263,120. He arrived at it by multiplying his net operating income by a factor of 11. The buyer countered with $30,000 under that price.

"Brad," said Bill, "what did I just tell you?"

"Come on," replied Brad. "Don't give me a hard time. The buyer wants to do the best he can."

"Brad, I wasn't kidding," said Bill. "Don't rattle my chain here!"

The next week Brad came back with a full-price *cash* offer. The sale took place on December 13, 1990. Bill paid off all loans against the property, all miscellaneous costs, and Brad's 3 percent commission (negotiated down from 6 percent because Bill is a broker himself and no other brokers were involved).

Bill walked away with $74,000 cash.

Adding this $74,000 to the $40,000 cash he received when he refinanced five years earlier, Bill realized that this single investment had yielded *$114,000 plus a substantial cash flow over the years*—all this after having put none of his own money into the deal, and having spent very little of his time managing it.

A Done Deal

"I've done several deals like this, many of which look like they're going to be even bigger money-makers," states Bill. "But I chose this as my 'best' deal because it's finished, and I can see exactly how many chips are left on the table."

CHAPTER 11

Heavenly Profits from a Church

In 1985, early in John Ross' real estate investing career, he came upon an interesting classified ad. It said that a church was for sale.

It turned out to be a solid brick building on a corner lot in Rochester, New York, John's town of residence at the time. (He now lives in Atlanta, Georgia.) It had an upstairs and a downstairs. The church was housed in the downstairs area. The reverend, a woman, lived in the upstairs portion of the building.

Initially, John couldn't believe that the asking price was only $35,000, especially because the address placed it in the same general area where he had his office—a nice area.

The No Zone

His research revealed why the price was so low: there were two glaring problems with the property. First, there was no parking other than what could be found on the street. Second, the property was not zoned to be a church. Nor, for that matter, was it zoned to be anything else.

"It actually had no legal zoning whatsoever," explains John, "which is why it wasn't selling. No one wanted to take it to the zoning

41

board. In fact, I found out that it had *never* had any zoning . . . at least that anyone knew of. They didn't have any record of it ever being zoned for a duplex, a church, a store, even for a single-family residence. It was the strangest thing I'd ever seen. There were absolutely no zoning records. Whether they'd lost them, or what, I don't know.''

Daring to go where others apparently feared to tread, John decided to buy the property and take on the zoning board. "I had never in my life gone up before a zoning board," he admits. "This was my first shot. But the way I looked at it was that this house was up for sale for about $35,000, and if I could negotiate the price down even further—which I knew I could do—I didn't have much to lose and probably had a lot to gain."

John was successful in his negotiations. How successful? Try a sales price of $19,000 cash. "I figured that I could at least fix it up as a single-family residence," he says. "That would give me a property worth $60,000 or $65,000. I had my own people that did this, and for every dollar I put into a property this way, I'd usually get above five dollars out."

The only catch was that John was cash-poor at that time, his liquid capital having been absorbed by a number of other recent real estate investments. So after negotiating the incredibly low price, he also negotiated incredibly favorable terms: a small deposit in the form of a promissory note to hold the property for three months. At the end of the three-month period, there would be a closing, at which time he would have to pay the $19,000 cash, or lose his deposit.

John went to work immediately to pull everything together before the end of the 90-day period.

Angels on the Zoning Board

First, there was the zoning dilemma. He knew he could make a good return on his money by converting the church into a single-family residence. But he also knew he could multiply those profits by getting the property zoned for multi-family residential usage. So, taking a deep breath and ignoring the horror stories he had heard about zoning boards, he took the plunge.

"I went before the board with my lawyer and my foreman, and we told them we wanted to make the church into a fourplex," John recalls. "We would divide it right down the middle, and between floors. We told them about our other properties, and showed that they were all well-maintained and up to code. We also took in about fifteen affidavits that we'd gotten from the people that lived around the old church that said they'd be in favor of us changing it into a fourplex. (They were relieved that we only wanted to put a fourplex there, rather than leave it as a church, or convert it to a corner store or small commercial building.)

After I presented the proposal I waited for the board to tear us apart, throw us to the lions, or at least call the guards and have us dragged away. But it didn't happen that way. They calmly asked me to draw up some plans and promised that they'd take my request into consideration. It wasn't at all what I'd been led to expect."

John had his people draw up some rough plans showing how the building would be divided, and where the various rooms would be. He submitted the plans to the board, and to his utter astonishment, they told him they would approve the fourplex if he would put in one parking space on the property.

"They said that normally, they would require two parking spaces per unit," says John. "But because it was on a corner lot, with parking on the street, all we had to do was put in one parking space. *They asked me if that would be okay.*

"I was so surprised and relieved, I almost fell down. It was like hitting the lottery. What the other potential buyers had been so afraid of turned out to be a gold mine. We had expected all sorts of flack and tremendous costs. We never expected the board to agree. I was elated. You see, I knew what I could sell it for if I could get it zoned as a fourplex. After putting $20,000 to $25,000 into fixing it up and dividing it up, I knew it would be worth anywhere from $120,000 to $130,000, because each unit would rent realistically for $450 a month."

Adding the parking space was an easy and inexpensive task. John instructed his crew to take out a rectangle of lawn (where people had been parking anyway), replace it with gravel, and put in a couple of railroad ties as a border. That was that. They got the new zoning.

Pennies from Heaven

The second thing John had to line up to make this particular deal fly was financing. He needed $19,000 cash to consummate the purchase by the time the closing date rolled around, plus enough money to have his crew do the necessary remodeling and fix-up work to convert it into a fourplex that would command the level of rent it was capable of.

Always ready to use a challenge as an excuse to parlay a big win into a bigger win, John took this deal to its profit limits by finding a Kodak executive in the area that was looking for an attractive real estate investment.

According to John, "We went to him and said, 'Look, we're going to turn this place into a fourplex; we're going to make it brand new; we're going to fill it up with tenants for you who will pay $450 per month per unit so you'll have a positive cash flow; and we're going to sell it to you for $15,000 less than whatever it appraises for when it's finished. And we'll do all this for a $50,000 down payment *up front.*"

The executive jumped at the chance.

The $50,000 down payment gave John the cash to pay the $19,000 purchase price and left him with $31,000 to cover the remodeling costs, which ended up running less than $25,000.

When John was finished getting the property ready to turn over to the Kodak executive, it appraised for $125,000 (by the appraiser at the executive's bank). So the final sales price, with the $15,000 discount, was $110,000 Since the executive had already paid John $50,000, he gave him a check for the remaining $60,000.

"I was in and out of the deal in a matter of approximately two months," explains John. Except for the time I put into it, it didn't cost me anything out-of-pocket. I walked away with the $60,000 from the final sale to the Kodak guy, plus over $6,000 that was left over from his initial $50,000 payment after construction costs.

"That's more than a $66,000 profit on a zero-dollar investment in about two months! It was a wonderful deal. And it was good for the executive, too, because he got a solid rental property with a good cash flow for $15,000 under the appraised value."

In addition to turning an excellent profit, the church property taught John three important lessons. First, it *is* possible to find excellent deals in properties that are already listed. Second, you *can* get into property investments even if you don't have the money to buy them. And third, zoning boards *aren't* necessarily the monsters they're cracked up to be.

The Best Deals
Aren't Always Spectacular

A very rich man was once asked how he made his money.

"I manufacture and sell pop bottle caps," he said. "I make a half penny profit per cap."

"How can you get rich making a profit of only a half penny per cap," queried the interviewer.

The rich man smiled. "Because I make five million of them a day."

This anecdotal account illustrates the important business concept that per-unit profits don't have to be spectacular to make you rich *if* you produce and sell enough units.

Willie Boyd, who began investing in real estate with his wife years ago, as a way to supplement his regular paycheck, has put this principle to work.

Residents of the college town of Durham, North Carolina, the Boyds currently own a large and growing portfolio of rental homes. Individually, none of their properties are spectacular in terms of size, value, equity position, or cash flow. But collectively, they have given the Boyds a very nice total equity position that gets bigger and better every month, plus a modest positive cash flow that will become a waterfall of profits when the mortgages against the properties are paid off.

45

A Basic Recipe

Because Willie follows the "cookbook" approach to investing (basically doing the same deal over and over again with different but similar properties), his "best" deal could be almost any of his investments. He selects the second rental house he bought—the Plum Street property—because it is representative of most of his portfolio.

"In 1982, my wife located the house in a local real estate listings publication," says Willie. "It was close to one of the two-year technical colleges in town—the Durham Technical College. The house is an 800 square-foot, two-bedroom cottage with a living room, a kitchen, and a big lot. But it needed cosmetic work. We had to go in and clean up, paint, clean up the yard . . . it was a real mess."

The home was listed for $22,000. Willie offered $14,000, and ended up buying it for $16,000.

"The interesting thing," recalls Willie, "was that we signed a contract to purchase the property in September of 1982, but we couldn't close until April, 1983, because we had trouble getting all the signatures. It was an estate property, and one of the heirs was in prison or something like that.

"We didn't have any money, so we went to the bank and got a 90-day, interest-only commercial loan for $19,000 to cover the $16,000 purchase price, the closing costs, the interest on the loan for three months, and about $2,000 in anticipated fix-up costs."

The bank needed collateral for the loan, of course. The rental house itself provided $12,000 of it (75 percent of the $16,000 sales price, which the bank used as the fair market value). The Boyd's automobiles were used to secure the remaining $7,000 of the loan.

Willie took the $19,000 loan, paid the total $16,000 sales price for the house, paid $400 in closing costs, paid $460 in interest on the 90-day note, and put just under $2,300 into fixing up the property. This meant that the project dipped about $140 into Willie's pocket.

Do-It-Yourselfers

The Boyds did the clean-up/fix-up work themselves, which he claims was the key to making this deal fly. It took less than three months to get everything done, working after regular working hours and on weekends.

According to Willie's plan, the property was rehabilitated and reappraised early enough to be able to refinance it in time to pay off the commercial loan when it came due at the end of the 90 days.

Its after-fix-up appraised value was $26,000—$10,000 more than what he had purchased it for, and $7,000 more than the total cost of buying and rehabilitating it. In short, the work the Boyds had put into the property earned them $7,000—a much higher dollar-per-hour rate than Willie earned in his regular job with General Telephone & Electronics (GTE).

The $26,000 appraisal came as no surprise to Willie. Not a man to take blind risks, he made a careful assessment of costs and values before getting into this investment. "It *was* a risk, of course," he says, "because it was just our second property. But we had a pretty good feel for what we were doing. What I did was to get a friend of mine who is an appraiser to do a 'before and after' type thing on the property. He told me what its value was as it stood when I was thinking of buying it. Then I told him what I would do to fix the place up, and he told me what the value would be after it was done. So I felt pretty comfortable about it."

And he had reason to be comfortable. His appraiser friend's estimates were right on.

With the new $26,000 appraisal, Willie refinanced the property at a local savings and loan with a 30-year mortgage. They gave him a loan of 80 percent of appraised value, or $20,800.

With these funds, Willie paid off the $19,000 commercial note plus $800 in closing costs, and paid himself back the $140 he took out of his pocket to pay the overrun on fix-up costs.

"So we ended up with about $860 in cash profits," he states. "And if you look at the equity position, we were sitting there with a $5,200 equity in the property."

That's a $6,060 gain—not bad when you consider that Willie only put $140 of his own money into the project, and that was paid back within a few months.

Just a Beginning

But that's not the end of the story. The house, which began renting for $297 a month, has yielded a modest postive cash flow from the start. This means that the renters are not only paying down the mortgage for the Boyds (which builds up their equity), but are giving them a little cash each month to boot.

In 1986 Willie refinanced the Plum Street house once again to take advantage of lower interest rates. His goal was to pay off the loan in a shorter number of years, rather than to take cash out of the property or to increase cash flow by lowering the monthly payments.

The lower interest rate allowed Willie to achieve his goal, cutting over 10 years off the life of the loan, and structuring monthly payments at a level that would still give him a modest positive cash flow.

The market value of the rental house today has climbed to $41,000. It pulls in $370 per month in rents, with hardly any vacancy problems. With all expenses accounted for—even a vacancy factor thrown in—it pays for itself and then some.

And best of all, the mortgage will be paid off in about ten years, leaving the Boyd's with a *plus* of a property free and clear.

CHAPTER 13

Relationships You Can Take to the Bank

C raig Horton's best deal involves a duplex and several good relationships.

By the end of 1988, this Medford, Oregon real estate entrepreneur already had 13 years worth of experience under his belt in the income property business. It was at this time that his wife, Jane, who had been born and raised in the Philippines, found a gem of a deal.

"My wife knows a lot of Filipinos in this area," says Craig. "One of them, a lady, owned a duplex here in Medford that she wanted to sell. It was a townhouse duplex with wood siding and a total of 1,800 square feet. She talked to my wife about buying it because she wanted to be cashed out. She needed money and felt that we might be able to come up with it.

"So we negotiated with her, and as it ended up, we told her that we'd pay $30,000 cash for the duplex, contingent upon a property inspection. She agreed."

A Good Deal Upon Inspection

In accordance with the contingency, Craig asked his father to go over to the property and inspect it with him. "My dad has been in the business for a long time," explains Craig. "He has owned a lot of units, and has helped me in the business. We went through and he inspected both units completely. We found that the seller had put a new roof and nice new wood siding on the building and had rewired it within the previous two years."

Craig's father confirmed what Craig had suspected all along: that the duplex was worth substantially more than the $30,000 cash purchase price. "You're getting a really good deal here," he said.

The next step involved getting the $30,000 to make the cash payment for the purchase. This was no problem. "I talked to my banker at Valley of the Rouge Bank," recalls Craig. "I made arrangements with him to get a $33,000 first mortgage loan on the duplex. It would be an interest-only quarterly payment loan with a one-year term.

"My father and I had done this many times before with Valley of the Rouge bank. We had a large line of credit, and we would go to them and say, "We're buying this property at a heavy discount. We want you to put a first mortgage on the property, and we will refinance within a year.' The bank loves those loans."

Next, Craig drafted an earnest money agreement for the $30,000 cash purchase, and took it to the title company, along with a small deposit. A closing date was set in a few weeks.

At the closing, the $33,000 first mortgage loan Craig received from the bank was used to pay the seller her $30,000 sales price, plus closing costs. When everybody and everything was paid, Craig walked away with a check for $1,141.

Craig owned the duplex at that point, which had a $33,000 mortgage on it. He also had a check for $1,141. But he couldn't rest on his laurels.

First Things First

First, he had to turn his attention to the duplex itself. One side of the property, which housed the granddaughter of the seller (who wasn't paying rent), had to be filled with a solid, rent-paying tenant. Plus, a few improvements had to be made, such as the replacement of a refrigerator and stove. All in all, this cost about $2,000. But by the time he was finished, he had a duplex that was in top shape and filled with solid tenants. One side rented for $300 a month, and the other (the side with the new tenant) rented for $335, for a gross rental income of $635.

Craig's second task was to find long-term financing to take the place of the one-year mortgage note from the Valley of the Rouge Bank.

"It was kind of a quirk thing," recalls Craig, "but a friend of mine that had just gone to work for a mortgage company called me and asked me if I knew anyone that wanted to refinance a non-owner occupied property. He said they had mortgage money available for that type of property. This was in the summer of '89, well before the one-year note was due. So I told him the criteria that I needed—what I had to have and what the restrictions were.

"You see, the problem was—and is—that it's tough to get decent financing if you own a lot of rentals. Because if you own more than about five or six units, your loan isn't salable on the secondary market. They really frown on it unless they 'portfolio' your loan, which means they keep the loan in their loan portfolio and don't try to sell it on the secondary market.

"My friend did some checking and found out that the loan *would* be a portfolio loan, so they could give me what I was looking for—a fixed-rate, long-term mortgage."

A Profit Already

The loan was for $35,000. This was based on the mortgtage company's June '89 appraisal, which had come in at *$50,000*. Remember, Craig bought it for $30,000 just seven months before that time. That's $20,000 in just over a half-year!

The loan was a 30-year first mortgage loan at a fixed interest rate of 10½ percent. Principal and interest payments were (and are) $320 per month.

Says Craig: "This is one of the best mortgages I've ever gotten. In this area of the country, it's really hard to get a long-term, fixed-rate, non-owner occupied mortgage, especially with the S&L crisis. Most of the mortgages you get now for non-owner occupied properties, if you own any rentals at all, are variable rate mortgages."

Of the $35,000 proceeds from the mortgage loan, $33,000 went to pay off the Valley of the Rouge Bank note, $1,225 went to closing costs, and $999 went to understructure work on the duplex that the lender insisted on as a condition of making the loan.

This left Craig with a bill for $224, which together with all other expenses that had gone into the property since Craig had originally bought it (also taking into consideration the $1,141 he took away from the original $33,000 loan), came to a total out-of-pocket cost of approximately $2,000.

In other words, when Craig walked out of the closing for the $35,000 refinance mortgage, he had a $35,000 mortgage and had spent a total of $2,000 of his own money on the project since the inception.

The Downs and Ups

That's the downside. "Here's the upside: Craig owned a property that was worth $50,000. (With the $35,000 mortgage, this gave him an equity position of $15,000—a figure that would grow larger as the mortgage was amortized and the property value increased.)

In addition, the duplex was generating a positive cash flow each month, with very few vacancy problems. Today, it is bringing in total monthly rents of $690, and is generating a positive monthly cash flow of $100 to $150 ($690 minus the $3209 mortgage payments minus other expenses). "This is a conservative figure,' admits Craig. "You've got to figure in reserves for repairs, vacancies, and all that."

Says Craig: "One of the major reasons why this deal came about was that my wife and I have a good working relationship in our real estate investments. She did a lot of the groundwork on this and helped put the transaction together. I really believe in the husband-and-wife partnership. Because of the fact that she's Filipino, and the gal that was selling the property was Filipino, it came together. They even talked the language when we were negotiating."

Another key to this deal as the $33,000 loan Craig received from the Valley of the Rouge Bank. Without it, he wouldn't have had the cash to purchase the property when the deal was hot, and without the cash, he wouldn't have gotten the kind of price he got.

"You've got to have a good relationship with a lender," Craig points out. "Not everybody can walk in and get that kind of money, and get it that quickly, with so little hassle. If you really cultivate a relationship with a bank, it can be done. But it takes awhile.''

These were not the only relationships that contributed to making this a "best" deal for Craig. His relationship with his father, an experienced veteran of the business, allowed him to call on his expertise when he needed to inspect the property. And his relationship with a friend resulted in a call that led to an excellent long-term mortgage loan.

When it comes right down to it, relationships are what the real estate investing game is all about. If you doubt it, ask Craig.

CHAPTER **14**

Having His Cake and Eating It Too

Bob Chilton was a banker for close to a decade. During those years, he created and ran a company that many investors would have been proud to have as their sole business and income source.

"While I was working at the bank," the Charleston, West Virginia investor explains, "I also built up a little company called Chilton Realty and Development Company. My father, Edward Chilton, who has been in this business since the '30s, and my brothers and sisters were my partners. We started out with a duplex, then added two different fourplexes, an 18-unit apartment building, and another 11-unit building. This all happened between 1969 and 1976. So we wound up with about 39 units in the company. It was fun.

"I got involved in real estate at an excellent time in this area," explains Bob, "partly because of inflation, and because the rental market was certainly good."

In Pursuit of Income Properties

If anything, this is an understatement. In the separate purchases, Bob paid a total of $342,000. Dividing that figure by 39—the numbers of rental units involved—you get a per-unit purchase price

54

of $8,769, which is a very good price for the kinds of properties he bought.

In 1976, things were clipping along very well for Bob's 39 rental units. They were in good shape, thanks to his property management skills and vigilance. They were generating healthy, positive cash flows. And their overall values had inflated substantially beyond their purchase prices.

In fact, because things were going so well, Bob was able to quit his banking job in '76 and dedicate his full time to pursuing his income property business.

This is where the plot thickens.

To properly understand this story, it is important to know that the Chilton family was also part-owner of a larger real estate company called Kanawha Village Apartments Inc. (The Chiltons owned 25 percent of the company—the largest ownership block in the corporation.) The corporation had been formed when Bob's father and five friends purchased the Kanawha Village Apartments in 1951 for $1.1 million in borrowed funds. Subsequent purchases had increased the size of the property portfolio.

In January of 1977, Bob engineered a transaction that provided very attractive benefits not only to his family, but to other shareholders of Kanawha Village Apartments: He sold the corporation his 39-unit block of rental properties for $635,000, which represented a fair market value at that time, as appraised by an uninterested, qualified third-party appraiser.

Remember, Bob had spent $342,000 to purchase the properties. Plus, he had invested approximately $50,000 more to improve them (he's a stickler on quality). When these amounts were deducted from the $635,000 sales price, Bob and his family company could sit back, calculator in hand, and bask in the realization that they had achieved a $243,000 profit—not to mention the positive cash flow they had been receiving for years from the properties.

Your Cake and Eating It

In reality, Bob and his family received much more than their $243,000 profit from the sale, because the underlying mortgage loans on the properties had been paid down over the years, and at that point only amounted to roughly $200,000. Kanawha Village Apartments, Inc. assumed these loans and borrowed the money to pay off the balance—over $400,000—in cash.

"We took that," says Bob, "paid our capital gains tax, and divvied up the money."

Why did Bob want to sell his properties to the corporation? In his own words: "It was an opportunity to realize an excellent capital gain. Plus, it allowed me to sell the properties and still own part of them while continuing to play a role in their management. Also, the corporation could take better advantage of the depreciation than we could. And our bank loans were down to where we had a large amount of equity, and were paying something like $40,000 a year in corporate income taxes."

Because the Chiltons were the majority owners of the Kanawha Village Apartments corporation, and because Bob was the most likely candidate to assume leadership of that entity, he was elected to be the president and chief executive officer.

"It's sort of like having your cake and eating it too," he remarks.

Almost ten years later, the Chilton family, under Bob's leadership, bought out the other shareholders. The Chiltons now own the corporation and its portfolio of close to 300 rental units exclusively.

That's a lot of cake.

Remembering That First Magic Deal

"The first deal of my life wasn't the one that made me the most money," says real estate investor/lecturer/author Barbara Kalb. "But I'll always think of it as my *best* deal because it was the most significant . . . and the one I remember as if it happened yesterday."

Back in 1973, when the Vietnam War was finally going away and John and Yoko Lennon were still making headlines, 21-year-old Barbara Kalb was a recent graduate from the University of Michigan.

"My husband and I were newlyweds," she explains. "We were living in government-subsidizied housing, which had been perfect for two poverty-stricken college kids. One Sunday, I picked up the *Homes for Sale* section of the newspaper and started looking through the classifieds.

"What possessed a 21-year-old to pick up the Sunday paper and start looking for a home, I will never, ever know. I mean, the audacity of me to think that we could buy a house after just graduating from college!

"I don't really believe in destiny, but I *do* believe that in some mysterious way, people are attracted to the things they are good at."

Whatever the reason, Barbara found herself scrutinizing a classified ad for an old duplex that was for sale that was being sold out of an estate. The asking price was $23,500, which was a lot more money in 1973 than it is today.

An Interesting Property

Recalls Barbara: "I said to my husband, 'Come on, Jim, let's just go drive by it.' We did, and it looked pretty interesting from the outside. By *interesting,* I mean *beat up.* But it was in a good section of our town (Dearborn, Michigan)—a nice, older neighborhood where the homes were mostly rentals. It wasn't a traditional side-by-side duplex. In fact, it looked like a regular single-family house, but it had a hidden back stairway leading upstairs to a smaller apartment.

"We called the real estate agent who had it listed. When we went through it, I had a feeling that something was clicking inside me. The moment I walked in, I started thinking, 'If only it had new carpet. . . . If only this arch were removed from the entrance to this little tiny room off the kitchen. . . . If only we could get a certain amount of rent from the upstairs unit to make enough to pay our house payment, then we could live in the downstairs for free. . . '

"All those thoughts just came to me, magically, as I walked through the house. I don't know why they occurred to me. I knew nothing about real estate. I didn't have an art background, and I wasn't a decorator by any means."

Call it intuition. Call it vision. Call it an innate awareness. But whatever it was, Barbara had it.

"When I give my talks around the country," she states, "I always say that the investments that require vision are the best investments, because you can use your vision to change things, then resell the properties to people that don't have vision."

The duplex that Barbara and Jim were looking at definitely demanded vision. But it also displayed another sign that Barbara intuitively knew would contribute to making it a profitable investment: it was vacant. "When a house is vacant, the sellers are paying the heating bills in the winter and they're paying someone in the summer to come and cut the grass," she explains. "This is especially true when a house is in an estate. You know there's somebody being bothered by the dead person's house. I didn't really *know* all this at the time. I just had certain feelings about it."

Although the Kalbs felt that the $23,500 asking price was a fair one, they did what any entrepreneurs worth their salt will do and offered less—in this case, $20,000. Plus, Barbara asked for a few other minor considerations.

"I thought to myself," she says, "that if we made a $5,000 down payment, then put the balance on a *land contract* (the term in many areas for a seller-carried contract where the seller takes back a mortgage for part of the purchase price), and tell the guy we'll pay him off in a year, in that year we can fix it up and get a mortgage for more than we paid for the house."

The seller accepted. Payments for the $20,000 mortgage were set up on a regular 30-year amortization schedule, but the entire note was to be due and payable at the end of a year.

"Looking back at it, it's funny that I knew about creative financing before anyone ever taught me anything about it. This was prior to the days when weekend seminars about investing in real estate and creative financing were going around the country. Somehow, I just figured it out.

"People in Michigan may not like me for saying this," Barbara laughs, "but I think I may have invented the balloon payment in the state of Michigan."

A Nothing-Down Deal

She may also have pulled off one of the few no-down-payment real estate transactions in her city that year. "For me, it was a nothing-down deal," she points out, "because as soon as we signed the papers, we knocked on my father-in-law's door and said 'Hey, Dad, give us five grand.' So we used other people's money for the whole thing."

Barbara explains that this was the first of many times they borrowed money from Jim's father. He welcomed this because he could generally get a higher interest rate from Barbara and Jim than he could get from a certificate of deposit. In every case, however, everything has been transacted in a written, business-like fashion, which Barbara says is imperative if misunderstandings are to be avoided—especially when dealing with family members or friends.

Both Barbara and Jim had each just signed teaching contracts for a whopping $8,000 a year, and were feeling extremely rich. "For us," laughs Barbara, "that was rolling in the dough. So we agreed to pay Jim's dad back at the rate of $350 a month. With paying back the $5,000 and making payments on the $20,000 loan, we were putting a lot of our monthly income into that house—probably triple the percentage that most couples can comfortably pay. But that was nothing to us because we had been used to living on virtually nothing.

"Still, it was an enormous jump. But you know, when you're young, and you suddenly graduate and get a good job, all that new money has got to go somewhere. And young people aren't usually disciplined enough to start socking it away in a savings account. If we hadn't had the house to put the money into, we probably would have bought stereo systems, trips to the Bahamas . . . money disappears because the urge to spend is there. But we got into the habit right from the start of putting our money into things that would bring us a return *without even realizing it*. We were satisfying our shopping urge and making a great investment at the same time."

Bringing It Up to Snuff

The Kalbs moved into the main downstairs apartment and went to work, devoting every spare minute after teaching school and on weekends and holidays to cleaning up, repairing, and improving the duplex. "I used to marvel at people who had time to just putz around," says Barbara. "We didn't have that, but it was a choice that we made, and I believe it strengthened our marriage."

They did all the work themselves that didn't require special skills. This was the bulk of the work. The rest, such as wiring, they hired out. They also had some free manual labor, supplied by volunteers from Barbara's high school classes who enjoyed being around this vivacious teacher who was just a few years older than they were.

They first worked on the upstairs rental unit, converting it from a $95-per-month to a $135-per-month apartment. This $135 came in handy when they had to make the mortgage payments each month. Then they focused on the downstairs area. The job took time and effort, but when it was finished, it was well worth it.

Before the one-year balloon on the $15,000 seller-financed mortgage came due, Barbara arranged for a long-term mortgage on the property. An appraisal was necessary, and Barbara and Jim realized what a great investment of time and money they had made when the appraisal came back at approximately $30,000—a full $10,000 more than they had purchased the duplex for just one year earlier!

The bank loaned the Kalbs a little more than $25,000 on the property in the form of a 30-year mortgage at an 8 percent interest rate. Barbara's plan had come to fruition.

With the refinanced loan proceeds, they paid off the seller's mortgage, now slightly less than the original $15,000, paid off the small remaining balance on the father's loan, paid themselves back for the relatively minor expenses they had incurred while renovating the house, and had some cash left over.

Let's Do It Again

The experience was so exhilarating that they decided to do it again. Two months later they moved out of their duplex and rented out the downstairs where they had been living for $250 a month. That meant that the total monthly rental income totaled $385. Because their mortgage payments were only about $185 per month, this left them with a very healthy cash flow—almost twice what they had been paying in rent before they bought the property. And as they raised the rents over the years, the cash flow got better and better.

Roughly six years later, the Kalbs finally sold this little money machine for $44,000, having more than doubled their investment in terms of property value alone. "Of course, we can't say we doubled our money," laughs Barbara, "because we didn't put any money into it."

If you believe in reincarnation, there is a plausible explanation for Barbara's seemingly intuitive real estate investment savvy, her success with the first investment, and her subsequent distinguished track record in the income property business: she was a rich and cunning real estate mogul in her last incarnation.

If you don't believe in reincarnation, you may be able to rationalize her success simply by saying "She's smart and willing to pay the price." This can't be denied. "Any money we made, we immediately bought another house with it or started fixing up another house," she explains. 'It's not like we parked our money in a bank and admired our bank statement every night."

Barbara has often laughed and said, "Every time we'd get a hundred bucks, we'd buy a house." That isn't much of an exaggeration. Now, she and Jim can laugh all the way to the bank.

CHAPTER 16

The Four-Houses-for-the-Price-of-One Deal

When Bob Barrett rolled into the small town of Brevard, North Carolina ten years ago, he brought with him every material thing he owned: a pick-up truck and a few pieces of furniture. He also brought with him all his money—the net accumulated fortune of a lifetime of work: $1,000.

It was like being "born again" but in the material rather than the spiritual sense. Bob was 55 years old then, just divorced, and had no special trade or education to depend on. All he knew was that he wasn't getting younger, and he had to move fast to get himself financially secured.

Looking for Security

From his limited experience with the rental real estate business, Bob knew that investing in income property was the way to get the security he needed. "When a person doesn't have a lot of money, but wants security, rental properties are the way to go," he claims.

Bob began painting houses, preparing income tax returns, writing articles for various publications—anything he could do to get a few dollars together to stay alive and, hopefully, buy an income property investment. Luckily, his living expenses were minimal.

To those who are desperately seeking it, opportunity always appears—but usually in strange disguises. "I kept seeing a classified ad in the paper," recalls Bob. "It read: 'Four houses for the price of one! $18,500.' It must have run for months. Nobody would touch those things.

"Obviously, buying four houses for $4,625 each was a death trap, but I was desperate. I had to get *something,* and those houses were something I could handle, even though it was mighty risky. I was in a position where I had to fight my way up, with no cash and no assets."

Bob took the leap of faith and called the listing broker to see the four houses. "I found the houses were worth the price," he laughs. Rolled siding that simulated the look of brick was peeling off exposed wood. ("From three miles away, they almost looked like brick homes," quips Bob. The homes were small. Two were one-bedroom houses. The other had two bedrooms. The rooms were small. The insides were beat up. The roofs were so bad that the squirrels would get in and store nuts above the ceilings, which were so flimsy that the nuts had fallen through in a few places.

Good News, Bad News

In terms of occupancy, there was some good news and some bad news. The good news was that all four houses were occupied. The bad news was that the occupants were always drunk, and that it almost took mugging them to get their rents. One of the two-bedroom homes, for example, was renting for $75 a month, "paid in installments—whenever she could get the money," remarks Bob. The other homes were renting for $130, $140, and $140 . . . at least in theory.

"Beat up as they were," says Bob, "I could see the potential. I knew that even if I had a lot of trouble with tenants, I could break even at the worst."

Not surprisingly, the owner was a motivated seller. There were two mortgages on the properties, held by a local finance company. One was an 18 percent loan, the other a 19 percent loan. Bob agreed to the $18,500 sales price, assumed the mortgages, which totaled approximately $17,000, and paid the balance of about $1,500 as a down payment. (Enough to pay the sales commission and closing costs. He had managed to sock this away by taking handyman and painting jobs.)

Bob was now the not-so-proud owner of four rental homes. "Naturally," he says, "I tried to refinance. Two ancient appraisers from an S&L showed up about 8:30 one morning, found two men already drunk and a woman drunk and asleep on the bed. They told me later they would have refused to lend on those homes anyway, even without the drunks."

A Bootstrap Operation

In short, Bob had to make do and continue renting the homes as they were to low-quality tenants, struggling to collect rents, and barely breaking even in terms of cash flow.

Whenever he got a few dollars ahead, he would buy the materials necessary to improve the properties, and do the work himself. Gradually, little by little, the homes began to show signs of improvement. In the same way, he was able to slowly improve the quality of his tenants and inch the rents up. It was, he admits, a "bootstrap operation."

Bob persevered for four years and fortune smiled on his tenacity. "I got a windfall," he explains, "in the form of a gift from a relative, and a few thousand dollars from another deal. With this, I was able to get in there and pay off the mortgages. After that, of course, I was home free."

Bob points out that he could have done a lot of other things with the money. "But the one *right* thing to do was to get those mortgages paid off and give myself a perpetual money machine," he says. "I was just about sixty years old at that time and what I needed was security. I didn't need to see Hawaii. I didn't need to buy a new car. I just wanted to get that thing paid off and make sure that I was going to have some money coming in every year from then on."

Although Bob didn't have enough left over to fix up the properties after paying off the balances of the two mortgage loans, the fact that he didn't have to pay over $300 a month to the finance company meant that his cash flow skyrocketed, giving him the funds to make significant headway in renovating the houses. (All in all, he has spent between $7,000 and $8,000 on the four homes in improvements and repairs.)

Today, the homes are in excellent shape (he added nice wood lap siding and made other major improvements). They are currently worth an estimated total of over $60,000, are filled with good tenants that haven't moved or caused problems for a year and a half, and are generating a total rental income of $630 a month. The only expenses that have to be taken out of that are insurance and taxes ($40 per month), and the cost of an occasional repair, leaving him with a monthly cash flow in the $550 to $590 range.

Cash Cows

In short, Bob now has what he calls a "cash cow."

He explains: "That's a management term for something that you keep milking and getting a lot out of even though you don't have to put much into it.

"It occurs to me," Bob concludes, "that when you have a guy like Mark Haroldsen who puts $7 million into a beat-up apartment complex, it's not much different than someone like me who did the same thing, but on a much smaller scale. I was taking the same kind of risk he was, relatively speaking, and I probably had the same kind of feelings about it that he did.

"What's nice is knowing that there's a place for the little guys to do the same sort of thing on a small scale and make it pay off the same way it does for the big buys."

CHAPTER 17

How to Win When You're Losing

In Amarillo, Texas, there's an attorney who knows how to make money on real estate that's falling in value.

Magic? No. John Broadfoot is many things, but he is not a magician. What he *is* is a good criminal attorney that has been willing to use solid income property investing principles and hard work to get ahead in a very tough market.

"I have 20 houses now," he drawls. "They're between one third and halfway paid off. And what I'm getting ready to do is tell people how damn bad this real estate is.

" 'It's terrible!' I'm going to tell them. 'You sure ought to get rid of yours. And by the way, why don't you take my notes and my cash in trade on your depressed property?' "

A Blessing in Disguise

For this Amarillo trial lawyer, income property investing has been one of life's true blessings. He believes in it because he knows from personal experience that it works. Working at it only as a sideline to his law practice, he has created a very comfortable net worth.

But he didn't always have this belief in the value of real estate investments. He explains: "Years ago, I began to read in the airline magazine ads of a guy in a striped tee-shirt sitting on a fancy car telling me I could win my financial freedom.

"I kept reading that ad all over Texas as I flew around on Southwest Airlines. And for a year I would not order that book because I *knew* that guy was a phony! I *knew* that didn't work. *Nobody* could do those kinds of things."

Finally, the ads wore down John's resistance and he ordered Haroldsen's book. "I really did enjoy reading it—lawyer and all—because I'd never done any real estate law, just criminal and personal injury law. I didn't even know what an escrow agreement and a contract for deed were. I know how ignorant lawyers that don't oandle real estate are because I was one of them."

Still, John wasn't a believer. "You see," he explains, "I'm a lawyer. I'm a skeptic. I think people lie. When I read Mark Haroldsen's book, I thought he was lying. I thought nobody could do what he said you could do."

A Case of the Jitters

Fear was also a factor. "You're talking to a real person in Amarillo, Texas who was more scared to sign his name on a dotted line for a piece of real estate than he was to try a murder case!" admits John. "When I finally started investing in real estate, I had the jitters so bad that I could hardly sign my name."

But he did. And he prospered.

John's best deal illustrates some important points about investing in a depressed market—which the Texas market has undoubtedly been for several years now.

Here's the scenario: Back in 1982, John got a call from an old friend in Houston, who said he owned a five-bedroom home in Amarillo on which a tenant had taken a lease-option. But after not making payments for some time, the tenant had left, leaving the home in less than perfect condition. What could he do?

Getting Creative

John had an idea. He inspected the property, saw investment

potential in it, and decided to make an offer on it himself.

Through a series of negotiations with the seller, John worked out the price and terms. The terms were complex enough and creative enough that even the highest paid real estate lawyer would have been proud to have engineered the deal.

But when the smoke had cleared, John had purchased the house for $23,500, had carried $2,257 cash away with him from the September, 1982 closing, and had two mortgages on the property: one was a two-year first mortgage note of $4,000 held by a local bank; the other was a $20,250 second mortgage note held by the seller, who subordinated his interest to the bank.

John's creativity even extended into how he would pay off the seller's note. Because the seller was going to be retiring in a few years, John proposed that he pay him only $58.91 a month for the first two years while he was in the process of paying off the bank mortgage, then, when the bank's note was satisfied, he would increase the monthly payments to the seller to $344.79 per month for the next 15 years (12 percent interest). He knew he could keep the home rented for $350 a month, so this would help him avoid a negative cash flow situation while he was paying off two mortgages.

John increased his equity in the house by doing the clean-up and fix-up himself. The house had appraised for $25,000 in good condition, and it was deemed that it would take $4,500 to put it in "good and marketable condition".

"Now do you really think," says John, "knowing that I'm a cheap guy, that I'm going to spend $4,500 to repair a building when I could paint it and do the nailing and mudding and taping myself? No sir. And that's exactly what I did." To finance the cost of the materials for the work, he arranged a $1,000 credit from the seller to himself at closing.

After all was said and done, John bought the house, did some work on it himself, made some cash at closing (some of which he spent to go to a real estate convention in Lake Tahoe with his wife), and structured his debt service in a way that he would have a break-even cash flow. In other words, his tenants would buy the house for him.

Not long ago, something happened that benefited John. Things had been clipping along just fine when the original seller, who now had a first mortgage on the property since the bank's loan had long been paid off, got a divorce and his wife got the mortgage note. John explains: "She was a spendthrift and she needed some money. So I discounted the note, which had already been paid down to about $4,000, and paid her off completely. That gave me the property free and clear."

John is now considering "reaping the harvest" by using a 1031 tax-free exchange to trade the house and use it as leverage to add other rental properties to his portfolio. "I'm going to take my money," he says, "and move it without paying taxes if I can through a tax-free exchange, into the property of somebody else that's real depressed about how terrible the real estate market around here is."

How much is it worth today? "I'm going to guess," states John, "that in our market it may be worth $18,000 to $20,000 today."

Wait a Minute!

How can John call this his best deal if it's going to sell for thousands of dollars *less* than what he paid for it, and when it generated only a break-even cash flow during the years he owned it?

"It may be worth a little less than I thought it would be," he admits, "but it's worth a whole lot more than I paid for it."

He makes a case for this statement: "I used other people's money to acquire this house, got some cash at closing, got some great tax savings along the way, and never paid a dime of my money except for some vacancies and repairs. Now, if I put a few dollars of my own money into this house and I sell it this year for $18,000 or $20,000, how much return on my money have I made?

"In fact," laughs John, "I was just looking through my real estate papers this morning, and I said to my wife, 'Hell, honey, I didn't know life had been so good to us! I'm fixing you up so you're going to be a rich widow. I'm going to make you happy, and when I get through doing all these crazy things, we're going to go down to New Orleans and have some fun.' "

Case closed.

CHAPTER 18

"The Bank Paid Me $10,000 to Make a $180,000 Profit"

L ike the other investors featured in this book, St. Louis real estate entrepreneur Ron Pratt can look back on a career peppered with many excellent investments. Under such circumstancees, selecting one single "best" deal is a difficult task—almost like having to choose a favorite child.

The investment Ron finally selected involved six fourplexes in a St. Louis suburban subdivision called Wyndhurst, which he bought with a partner. The buildings were brick, two-bedroom townhouses. They were attractive, but the yards had been neglected for years. Trash was everywhere.

The subdivision, consisting of about 40 fourplexes, was developed by a builder who had sold off one fourplex at a time and was now down to the final six buildings. These were located right at the front of the development, behind the stone pillars at the entrance.

"A friend of the builder was managing the six fourplexes" explains Ron. "He was doing a lousy job, and consequently, less than half of the 24 units were occupied.

"I found out about the properties in 1986 through my networking grapevine. I was told that they were under contract, but the sales agent told me the contract was looking weaker all the time. The contract was for $300,000 or $50,000 per fourplex. I knew that with a little TLC and firm property management, each building would be worth about $85,000. I didn't want to miss such a good deal. You can imagine my excitement when the broker called me and told me that the contract had fallen through.''

In Cash We Trust

But Ron's excitement turned to panic when he was told that the seller, who was stinging from having the deal fall through, would now accept nothing less than an all-cash offer. In fact, he was demanding a $5,000 non-refundable earnest money deposit, a no-contingency contract, and a closing in 30 days, at which time the full balance would be due.

"I did have the $5,000,'' states Ron, "but to risk losing $5,000 of my closest friend's money, should I not be able to get a loan, was scary. I was being placed in a position of writing an all-cash contract and not having 'all cash.' "

Ron arranged a meeting with his banker, who met with him to look over the property. After the inspection, his banker said he would make a loan on the property equal to 62 percent of the appraised value, subject to board approval.

Ron figured he could fix up the properties before the appraisal was made, and that they would appraise for about $85,000 a piece, or a total of $510,000. Sixty-two percent of that amount would be $316,200, which would more than cover the remaining sales price balance, after the $5,000 deposit, of $295,000.

He recalls: "If my estimate of value was correct, I would end up at closing with a check for about $16,000, (less the closing costs) and have six buildings in my portfolio with a huge potential profit waiting for me.

"On the other hand, if I was wrong about the value of the property, and the appraisal came in for less than the expected $85,000 per building, it would require my putting cash down at closing. Or if the bank didn't approve the loan, I'd really be in trouble. These were real risks, because I was doing well to come up with the $5,000 cash earnest money. But I decided that the opportunity was too good to pass up, and I wrote the contract. It was accepted and I was on my way.''

A Ten-Day Clean Up Time

The bank scheduled the appraisal, giving Ron ten days to do what he wanted to do with the property. Here was another risk: he would have to clean-up and fix-up real estate that he didn't even own. The seller obviously had no problem with him doing so, but the task would take a lot of Ron's time and money (about $2,000)—all of which could go down the drain along with his $5,000 earnest money deposit if anything went wrong.

"I'm sure the owner was surprised when a 40-yard dumpster was delivered by a commercial hauler, followed by me and my quickly assembled crew," laughs Ron. "My wife, Joan, me, and four men spent four grueling, ten-hour days getting the landscaping in shape. We filled the dumpster twice to capacity with an amazing array of trash."

At the same time, Ron was trying to hedge his bets by finding someone to buy his contract, should he not be able to fulfill it. (He had no sure indication that the bank board would approve the loan.) Lining up a "take-out" contract buyer proved to be an easy task. In fact, buyers were lined up to take Ron up on his offer. This confirmed Ron's feeling that he was sitting on a gold mine. He arranged to sell the contract to an individual investor if he couldn't fulfill it for an amount that would give him a $5,000 overall profit on the deal.

But $5,000 was nothing compared to what he knew the deal would be worth, so even though he had protected himself against loss, his substantial gain was still in jeopardy.

The appraisal was made, and after a week of cruel suspense, Ron was told that his own estimate was right on: the property had appraised for $510,000. Still, the loan approval was necessary. It came just five days before the closing date.

Knowing that this was the last obstacle, Ron immediately launched his "blitz" of the property by contacting tenants to set up appointments.

The day of the closing came, everything went as planned, and after paying closing costs, Ron walked away with approximately $10,000 in his pocket. "I felt as though the bank had paid me to buy the property," he remarks.

Use the Profit and Do It Again

During the next 14 months, Ron and his partner improved the six fourplexes by applying solid property management techniques. At the end of that time, the property appraised for $90,000 per building—adding $40,000 to the investment pie.

Ron received a cash sales offer for the property at that time that would have given him a check for $180,000 in profits to split with his partner after all expenses of the sale were deducted. They debated whether to take it or not, because the fixed-up fourplexes had been generating an excellent cash flow. But they finally decided to take their profit and do it again.

"You know," conjectures Ron, "it's one thing to earn $90,000 in a regular job over a two- or three-year period. But it's an entirely different matter to suddenly have $90,000 in your savings account! As a lineman for a local utility company here in St. Louis, I can remember how hard it was to save $2,000 or $3,000. To suddenly have $90,000—well, let's just say it's as astounding to me today as it was back them."

Finding a Bargain by Finding the Need

A couple of years after his first real estate investment, Miami attorney Steve Wayner bought a single-family rental home that he considers to be the best deal he ever did, though certainly not the biggest money-maker.

Needs vs. Wants

"The reason why it was such a good deal," he explains, "is that it illustrates one of the five major keys that I've always claimed is important to a profitable real estate investment: finding out the sellers' *needs*—not their *wants*."

In 1982, Steve became interested in a house in Miami that a lady was selling for $65,000. There was a $25,000 first mortgage on the property, which meant that her equity was $40,000. She wanted the buyer to assume the mortgage and pay her the remaining $40,000 in cash.

"Obviously," states Steve, "putting $40,000 down to buy a $65,000 house with a $25,000 assumed mortgage wasn't a good deal. It was way too much to put down. I wouldn't have been getting any leverage.

75

"Although I told the lady that that was too much to put down, and that I couldn't buy the house because she wasn't willing to come up with some financing, I tried to keep talking to her.

"One day, when we were going through the home, I noticed that her daughter had a bunch of gymnastics trophies. I complimented the daughter and started talking about gymnastics, mentioning that my daughter at the time was taking a gymnastic class. The lady told me that her daughter was going to go to the University of Florida the coming year, and said that they don't give gymnastics scholarships."

The daughter then told Steve that it was going to cost $6,000 a year to put her through college at the University of Florida.

Recalls Steve: "Right after the daughter said that it was going to cost $6,000 a year to go to school for the next four years, the mother said, 'I'll take $24,000 as a cash down payment.'

"Now, when the mother said that, I knew I had discovered her need, because $6,000 times four years was obviously $24,000. So what she was doing was selling this house to pay for her daughter's college education. That was her need, and I had found it out by accident just because I had taken the time to talk to her."

A Future Need

Steve asserts that you can always ask sellers what their motivations are for selling properties, and they will often tell you. But what you hear may not be the real reasons. Perhaps they don't want you to know. Perhaps they don't even fully understand themselves what their true needs are. More often, they don't understand that there may be creative ways to finance a purchase that will better meet their needs and the buyers' needs.

"Now I knew this lady's need," states Steve. "That need was $24,000 to pay for college. But the need was not $24,000 *today*. The real need was $6,000 a year for four years. That was the need, and that was the offer I made: $6,000 a year for four years, with no interest accruing during that time, and the remaining portion of the debt (which in this case would be $16,000) to be paid off over ten years *after* the first four years had passed, at 10 percent interest."

Of course, Steve would have to assume the existing $25,000 first mortgage loan on the house. The interest rate on this long-term loan was 8¼ percent.

What this all meant was that for the first four years Steve owned the house, he had to pay $192 per month for the first mortgage loan (including taxes and insurance), plus an additional $500 a month for the second mortgage loan to the lady that sold it to him.

"This gave me a monthly payment of $692," says Steve, "and I rented it out for $700 a month, giving me a positive cash flow of $8. *But* I was paying down $6,000 a year in principal on the zero-interest second mortgage alone, so I was making a profit of $6,000 a year just on that, while I was also paying down the other $25,000 loan by about $900 a year.

"So I was making, in principal pay-downs, almost $7,000 a year, and getting a small positive cash flow at the same time, which is fantastic for one little house. When you buy something for $65,000, with no down payment, and you pay off more than a third of it in less than four years and get a positive cash flow, *that's* a good deal."

Steve points out that the reason this investment was so good was that, first and foremost, he had a $24,000 interest-free loan for the first four years, during which time he enjoyed accelerated equity build-up through accelerated principal pay-down.

Cash Flow Clincher

After that first four-year period, his $500 per month payment to the seller dropped to about $211 ($16,000 for 10 years at 10 percent interest). This fattened his positive cash flow by a substantial $289 per month!

But he didn't use this extra money for personal luxuries. Instead, like so many other successful investors, he chose to plow it back into his investment. He explains: "What I ended up doing was paying an additional $18,000 debt against it on the first mortgage. By that time, the rent had increased to $725 per month, and the property itself was worth about $74,000, giving Steve a $56,000 equity position.

"It hasn't really appreciated much," Steve admits. "And that's over quite a long time period. *But,* I have an advantage that a lot of other people don't: I now have a $56,000 equity in a property that I haven't had to put my own money into."

The clincher is the cash flow. With the second mortgage paid off, and monthly first mortgage payments of just over $200 (taxes have gone up a bit), Steve's positive cash flow is an endearing $500-plus a month (minus occasional repair and maintenance expenses, which have totaled no more than $3,000 in all the time he has owned it).

Plus, he hasn't had a day of vacancy since he moved a tenant in after buying the home.

"All of this is pretty good," says Steve, "because I got the property for a fair price. I didn't steal it, but I didn't over pay. And I told the seller, up front, that I would do this deal, but that she was not going to get a lot of interest. Usually, I like to get a *very* good deal when I buy a piece of property. In this particular case, I would normally have offered no more than about $55,000 for the house instead of $65,000 even though it may have been worth it. But I told her that since she wouldn't be getting a lot of interest, I'd pay the $65,000 asking price.

"I have a couple of other properties that I've earned a couple of hundred thousand dollars on," concludes Steve. "But from the standpoint of structure and driving home the importance of finding out the seller's needs, this was definitely my best deal."

Restoring Old Mansions for Fun and Profit

"In 1983 I left my job as a newspaper photographer cold-turkey," says Monroe, North Carolina's Rick Crider. "I was hell-bound to do something different. That's when I started paying attentin to old houses."

Rick was already an old home buff, having cut his teeth on them four years earlier when he bought and fixed up a stately old mansion in the heart of downtown Monroe. It was his personal residence, though—not an investment property.

Now he was looking for a new career, and he wondered if buying and fixing up old Southern homes—something he had both an aptitude and affinity for—might not fit the bill.

"One old house on Hayne Street that was just around the corner from where I was living caught my attention," he recalls. "I had literally driven by this house almost on a daily basis since 1977. But I'd never really paid attention to it until I started looking for that type of property.

"It was a huge, ugly mess right here in downtown Monroe. It had obviously been cut up into apartments because of the mailboxes and electricity meters. However, there was only one unit that ever looked occupied."

Tracking Down the Owner

Intrigued, and smelling opportunity, Rick went to the tax office at the courthouse early in 1984, looked up the property's records, and found out that it belonged to a woman named Mary Wiley Stewart, a woman in her eighties who had never been married. A different home address told him that she did not live in the old house.

Further research at the courthouse told Rick that Miss Stewart had inherited the house from an aunt in 1951. "That told me right there that she didn't have a dime in it, except what she had spent on repairs and maintenance, which obviously was very little," he says.

"Three of the four units in the house were empty and padlocked. The building was in rough shape. Windows were broken. There were squirrels and birds inside. It was a real mess."

A "Must-Have" Property

Beyond the mess, the house, which had been built in 1908, offered 5,400 square feet of interior space, had a huge wrap-around porch, was constructed of German siding, and followed the neo-classical architectural style (columns all the way around the front porch), with elements of the Victorian style.

Rich contacted Miss Stewart, told her who he was, and that he was interested in possibly buying her Hayne Street home. "My brother John and I met her over at the house in April," he says. (Rick's brother was an experienced real estate investor in Charlotte, and Rick had asked him to be there when they inspected the property.) "She fumbled around with the keys and eventually found the right one to let us in. I had admired the outside of the house, even in its rundown condition, but I didn't know what was in store for me inside.

"The moment I walked in, I was absolutely amazed and bowled over at the craftsmanship and the woodwork in that house! When I saw the staircases and the oak woodwork that had never been painted—just stained and varnished—I knew I had to have it. There was just no letting up at that point."

Miss Stewart was very cordial and talkative. She told Rick the long history of the house, which had been in her family since 1909, when it was purchased for $9,000 from the man who built it the year before.

The octogenarian spent almost three hours with Rick and his

brother that day, telling them stories about the house and showing them its many fine but dusty details.

"We had to help her up and down the stairs," recalls Rick. "Each and every room had a story. By the end of the day, I finally just asked her what it would take to buy the place. She hem-hawed around, but wouldn't name a price.

"She never would name a price, so in the coming months, I made several simplified written offers to her—offers she could take to her attorney. She valued his opinion. He was an older fellow here in town and had been doing her legal work for years."

Rick's first offer was for $36,000. She refused flatly. He began inching the offers up, a little at a time, over a period of several months, giving her time to take the offers to her attorney, but not so much time that she would forget that he wanted the home. He eventually offered as much as $55,000, if she would carry some of the financing.

"What it all boiled down to," explains Rick, "is that she had other plans for the place which she wouldn't tell me about. That's why she never would agree on a price."

A few months later, in September of 1984, Miss Stewart died. Rick found out because he happened to see the ambulance at her house. Sheepishly, he called her attorney, whom he knew by this point, and told him that he was still interested in the property, and that he'd like to be informed as soon as possible what was going to happen to it.

Invitation for an Offer

Within a week, the attorney told Rick that Miss Stewart had willed the house to Duke University Medical Center, suggesting that it be sold and that the proceeds be used for medical research.

Says Rick: "I immediately called Duke University's trust department and let them know they had inherited a house. I believe I told them before they ever got notice in the mail. I told them that the house was in bad shape, and that only one of the four apartments was habitable, and that that one was renting for only $75 a monthy. I also sent them some photographs showing details of the disrepair.

"Duke immediately thought about liability. I'm sure it occurred to them that they had this uninsured albatross of a house in a small town a couple of hundred miles away. So they were anxious to sell it.

As a matter of fact, nobody from Duke even came down here to look at the house.''

In the end, Duke University invited Rick to make an offer. He did: $26,000. They turned it down, and said that they would accept as a sales price whatever value the house was listed for at the courthouse, no questions asked. That price was $47,900.

Rick told Duke that because of the bad condition of the property, it would be tough to get financing on the house. Duke said, ''Fine, send us a 10 percent down payment and we'll finance the balance for 15 years at 12 percent interest.''

The deal was done, and the closing took place in November, 1984. Rick gave Duke a $4,790 down payment, and signed a mortgage that committed him to 15 years of $517 payments each month.

He immediately went to work on the old mansion, often working all through the night to get one of the units ready to rent. He did the work himself because he couldn't afford to pay anyone to do it (he was keeping body and soul together with fees from free-lance photography), and because he enjoyed it. The unit was ready in just over a month, and rented for $275.

Just after signing the closing papers, Rick had raised the rent on the sole tenant in the house from the ridiculous level of $75 to $150. This was an upstairs apartment. After a few months, the tenant moved out. This gave Rick the chance to remodel the unit. Once this was done, it began renting for $275. At this point, the home's rental income exceeded the monthly mortgage payments.

Next, Rick moved into the home himself. ''I had the two apartments fixed up and on line,'' he says, ''so I then took the other two apartments (the largest and nicest), tore out some of the divider walls, and consolidated them into my own personal residence.

''There was also an unfinished upstairs area with about 400 square feet and a separate entrance. I went ahead and finished it, making it into a little efficiency unit. It rented out for $235 a month.

''This didn't happen overnight. It was over about a year's time.''

A Showcase Property

All in all, Rick spent approximately $20,000 to restore and renovate the old home. When he was finished, he had a showcase property of which both he and the town of Monroe were proud. Plus, he had a large and beautiful personal residence, which he was living in for free, and a positive cash flow of about $300 a month, thanks to the rents from the other three apartments (he had raised them since he first rented them out).

Rick refinanced his Hayne Street home in 1987. An appraisal in June of that year indicated that the home was worth $136,500. That was $88,600 more than what he had paid for it two and a half years earlier!

The new mortgage loan was for $95,000. It was a typical 30-year, adjustable-rate loan, with monthly payments of $688. After paying off the existing mortgage held by Duke University ($40,400) and closing costs, Rick walked away from the loan closing with a check for $51,900. Even with the higher new monthly mortgage payments, he still had a positive monthly cash flow.

"I plowed the $51,900 back into my real estate investments," says Rick. "I spent about $12,000 of it to build a very nice 960 square-foot workshop-garage on the back of the house that matches it perfectly—right down to the trim. It's heated, air-conditioned, has a stereo, TV . . . it's like a little playhouse out there."

The garage added another $20,000 in value to the Hayne Street house, by Rick's conservative estimate, bringing the property's value up to about $156,000. Plus, Rick has continued to add various other exterior and interior updates and improvements to the home. Judging from the values of other homes in the area, he believes the current value of the house is $200,000.

Not a Boring Subject

The current total rental income is $950 a month. Rick admits that he could get more, but that he keeps rent levels low for his excellent, long-term tenants. The adjustable-rate mortgage payments are now up to $860, which means he still has a positive cash flow, and still lives there (now, with his wife) for free.

Rick is now in the process of having the house listed in the National Register of Historic Places, which will enhance the property from a standpoint of prestige and perhaps even value. It will also give him a 50 percent break on local property taxes.

Who says history is boring?

CHAPTER 21

All In The Family

" If I were to die today," reflects Florida real estate investor John Rudnianyn, "the deal I'd want to be remembered for is the one that I'm finishing up right now."

In 1984, John—who has been in the business since 1969—had the opportunity to help some people buy a piece of lakefront property on Lake Ker, near his town of Ocala (about 75 miles northwest of Orlando). It comprised roughly 33 acres of land, and had 1,700 feet of lake frontage. The price was $100 a front foot, or $170,000. Six parties were involved, including himself.

"It was a gorgeous piece of property on one of the most magnificent lakes you'll find anywhere," says John. The six partners bought the property for $170,000 cash, and divided it up as equitably as they could into six three-acre lakefront parcels. To figure out who got which parcel, they took six numbers, threw them into a hat, and drew to see who got which pick.

Selling Land to Smokey the Bear

This meant that 15 acres of the original 33 acres were left over after everyone got their lots. "I sold that 15 acres to the Forest Service," explains John. "The U.S. Forestry Service is required by law to pay the appraised value of any real estate they buy. It's crazy, but even if you were only asking $70,000 for a piece of property that appraises for $100,000, they'd still have to give you $100,000.

"They appraised our 15-acre parcel property for $4,000 an acre. (The property we were selling them was beautiful, but not as valuable as the 18 acres we were keeping.) So they said they'd give us $60,000 for the 15 acres, in round numbers."

But John wanted to try to get a little more for it, so he spent $250 to have a surveyor do a layout of the 15 acres showing how it could be divided up into one-acre lots. "Without doing anything more than just that $250 layout," he says, "the Forest Service appraiser looked at it again and reappraised it for $5,000 an acre, or $75,000.

"Because we got that money back, each of the six property owners—after brokerage fees, closing expenses, and everything—had less than $20,000 in his three-acre lakefront lot. That was a good buy even at that time."

How good of a buy was it? Two of the original six partners sold their lots immediately for about $60,000 each. Another split a one-acre parcel off of his lot, sold it for $30,000, and kept the remaining two-acre parcel.

A Family Business

Backing up a bit, it should be pointed out that although John did the deal, his lot was actually in his father's name. "We had purchased this lot not for him to sell, but to have it go through his estate," he explains, "because he's an older man."

So whose money actually bought the lot? John's or his father's? In answer, John says, "We run a diversified family investment operation. Everybody in my family—my parents, my wife, and my children (age 9, 12, and 15)—all own their own real estate themselves. The children have trusts and understand what they own. They wheel and deal with their real estate. They go out and work on their real estate. And so each entity in our family has its own operation, including my parents. And if someone needs money, someone else in the family always is there to make a loan. We loan among ourselves at 12 percent interest."

So the answer to the question "Whose money?" is fuzzy. John admits that he may have loaned his father the money to get into this particular deal. The fact that John did the deal himself, combined with the fact that the intention was to leave the property in his aging father's estate, makes it even fuzzier. But then, that's family life.

"My parents are Russian immigrants," John points out. "They made an average of about $5,000 a year. They lived on a chicken farm and grew everything. They never had much. They didn't need much. And they could survive on almost anything. If they made $5,000, they would save half of it. And because of compounding interest over a period of years, these people wound up with a bunch of money in the bank."

In the six years following the purchase of the lakefront property, its value rose substantially. A man from California, after visiting the lake and deciding that he wanted to buy the very best property on the lake (which happened to be John's lot and the one next to it) and build a half-million dollar home on it, made John and his father an offer. After some negotiations, they settled on a *cash sales price of $274,000.* After all costs and fees were paid, the Rudnianyns walked away with a check for a little more than $270,000. This took place in 1990.

Remember, their basis in the property was less than $20,000. Says John: "We structured a 1031 tax-deferred exchange under the current provisions where you have 45 days to select a property and 180 days to close.

This is Where the Plot Thickens

"We ran into an opportunity to buy a large block of land for $284,000," states John, "and with the exchange of the three acres of lake property plus an additional $20,000 to cover the balance and some closing costs, we ended up getting a little over 157.51 acres on the edge of the town of Ocala.

The property was part of a larger 409-acre tract of land. The seller was asking $7,500 per acre, but had reduced the price to $5,500 an acre. I was interested.

"I got a call from the broker at home one evening," recalls John. "He said he knew I was interested in the property. He said that the owners were wealthy. Now, my experience has taught me that there are two types of sellers that can make you good deals. One is the seller that needs the money so bad that he's got to sell. The other is the seller that's so rich that when he gets mad or bothered, he'll sell no matter what he gets.

"This particular seller was wealthy. He got tired of the property and just wanted to sell it. So the broker said, 'I think if you offered $1,900 an acre, he'd take it.' I have no idea where he got that figure.

"I went to bed that night, got up the next morning, called the broker, and said, 'Gus, I swear I had the craziest dream last night that you called me and said I could get that property for $1,900 an acre.' He told me it wasn't a dream, and I had a cash contract to him in a half hour.

"So now we have less than $40,000 in 157.51 acres that's worth about $6,000 an acre."

Push Opportunity to the Limits

That would be considered an incredible deal in anyone's book, but like other successful investors, John has learned to make a good deal even better, and push opportunity to its limits. Because the land he bought lies in the direction of Ocala's growth, he has had the 157.51 acres laid out into 70 residential lots that will sell for not less than $30,000 a piece. To get those lots developed, he will have to invest no more than $500,000. That includes the engineering, the roads, the underground electrical lines, wells, septic tanks, and so on.

It's calculator time.

At present, John has turned an investment of less than $20,000 into a piece of land conservatively worth $945,000—*almost 50 times the cost of the original investment.*

That part of it is a "done deal." But the near future holds even more promise. When the land is developed into the planned 70 residential lots, it will be worth $2,100,000. Deducting the approximate $500,000 cost of development, that will leave *a profit of $1,600,000.*

How did John do it? Its no secret: he knows exactly what he's doing and he knows his turf. "I develop a lot of land around here," he says. "I know all the land in this county. There are probably very few owners of any tracts of land of any consequence that I'm not familiar with.''

Knowledge. That's the key. Combined with the financial clout of a family of investors, knowledge can make real estate a powerful investment opportunity.

Profits on the Run

New Jersey real estate investor and writer John Koster claims that the best deal he ever did was also one of his fastest. "This was the one that wouldn't hold still for me," he quips. "I had to do it on the run."

Several months before this deal, John had informed a number of real estate agents and brokers that he was actively interested in anything in certain towns that was seriously underpriced and not too big. One day, after three days of heavy rain, John got a call at his home from a salesperson who said that she had something that he should see. "But it has to be fast," she added.

John put his writing project aside and drove to the property. It was only a mile away from where he lived. The sales agent was waiting for him in the rain.

"It was a house—an 1850s farmhouse, not old enough to be an historic home, and not new enough to offer a lot of conveniences," he recalls. "The rooms that had been decorated were done with garish hexagonal day-glow wallpaper. The effect was something between a hippie crash pad and the camouflage design on a World War I German fighter plane.

"That was the bad news. The good news was that this house was essentially sturdy, and that it sat on a lot that had almost enough area for a second house, even according to the town's very strict zoning ordinance."

Taking the Plunge

The asking price was $134,500. "This was in the '80s when property values were in a dizzy climb, sometimes going up 30 percent a year," John points out. "I knew that even if I couldn't get a minor subdivison approved to put up a second house, inflation would cover my closing costs and renovation expenses in a matter of a few months. So I took the plunge."

Because he was over invested at the time and cash poor, John brought a partner in on the deal. In fact, he drove right over to his office and told him that they could get into something good, but that they had to move fast unless they wanted someone else to snatch it up. They drove back, John showed the partner the property, and they negotiated a sales price of $133,500, knocking $1,000 off the asking price because there was water in the basement.

Shortly after signing the sales agreement, someone else made an offer of $137,000—$2,500 more than the asking price. "Those were crazy times," laughs John. The seller honored John's and his partner's contract, and they became the proud owners of the old home.

The closing date was late June, which turned out to be unfortunate timing, because John's partner had four children, had made commitments to special graduation activities, and wasn't able to do much of the renovation work at first. Says John: "I ended up doing a lot more work than I thought was fair with my own two kids, who were home-schooled and didn't have to bother with the non-academic frills. They could work when I did, and between us and my partner—once he got his schedule straightened out—we turned the appearance of the house around completely."

This included a new kitchen cabinet stained to match the existing one, a new tub/shower with sliding doors, new flooring in certain areas, new off-white paint job, plus everything else of a cosmetic nature needed for a complete clean-up/fix-up.

The result was a home perfectly suitable as a young couple's starter home, or an empty-nesters' alternative to a retirement community. "A prime-time, upscale, suburban house it would never be," admits John, "but it was eminently rentable, and I went out looking for a tenant on a one-year lease so I could sit back on that part of the project and let the house build up some equity with the help of the area-wide surge in real estate."

Room for One More

John's next step was to take advantage of the large lot. His plan was to apply for a minor subdivision (permission to split the existing lot roughly in half so a second house could be built. "This was made more probably because the house sat on one corner of the lot, leaving the other three corners unobstructed," he explains. "If I'd had a preternatural love of litigation, I could have tried to get a subdivision for three new lots and three new houses. But I wasn't that greedy."

A friend, who happened to be the building inspector, told John that he had a reasonably good chance of getting approval for the second lot and house as long as he handled it right, which meant not alienating the neighbors and asking for just the two-lot split, rather than four. And of course, he would have to refrain from losing his temper or doing anything socially unacceptable when he went up before the Planning Board—a body of appointed officials that approves or disapproves minor subdivision requests based on a mixture of legal qualifications, neighbors' input, and personal feelings.

"I got my first surprise at my first hearing," recalls John. "I'd had a licensed planner draw up a simple plan for what is called a *flat lot*—a housing lot with a narrow entrance leading to a full-sized square lot behind the existing house. But while the Planning Board and I thought this was the best plan from an aesthetic standpoint, the neighbors didn't like it.

"They wanted the new house to set cheek-to-cheek with the existing farmhouse. Although I disagreed with their sense of beauty, I realized that they had to live with it, while I only had to drive by it once in a while. So I told the Board I wanted to withdraw the plan and do a revision. The neighbors applauded."

A month later, John was back before the Planning Board with the new plan, as the neighbors had wanted it. To his surprise, some of them came to the meeting and praised him for taking their wishes into consideration. The result was a unanimous approval of John's minor subdivision request.

John and his partner now had a vacant lot worth about $100,000—which is what they sold it for just a few weeks later.

Totalling Up the Profits

A year later, after making essentially only cosmetic improvements, they sold the farmhouse (now on a smaller lot) for $159,000. That gave them another $25,500 profit, minus the costs of their improvements, which were minimal since they did almost all the work themselves.

Taking score, John and his partner made approximately $120,000 profit ($100,000 for the extra lot plus about $20,000 on the house) in just over a year on a $133,500 "spare time" investment.

"That was the best deal I ever did," John concludes. "I made money on the sale of the house. I made a huge amount of money on the creation of the minor subdivision, which involved a lot less sweat, swearing, and actual time than renovating the house, by the way. Although the vast, fast profits were partially the cause of the upsurging local economy, the principles can be widely applied: Move fast when you see a good value; do as many of the repairs as you can yourself; and listen to the neighbors—especially when they have clout with the local planning board."

CHAPTER 23

The Schoolgirl and Her Fourplex

Three years ago, when Tracy Fitzgerald was a mere 18 years old, she bought a fourplex for $110,000.

Why would a high school senior who didn't even have her own checking account buy a fourplex at a time in life when most girls' biggest financial concern is the cost of a prom dress?

The answer is simple: Her father and mother (both experienced rental property investor/landlords) encouraged her to do so.

"I wouldn't say I was *pushed* into it," laughs Tracy. "In fact, Dad tells me I definitely wasn't pushed. *Encouraged* is the word he uses."

Cutting Her Teeth in Real Estate

Tracy, the oldest child of Ed and Wendy Fitzgerald, had been working for her father—a fireman who buys and manages rental properties as a 40-hour-per-week "side" job—for a year and a half. Her job consisted of helping fix up and maintain the rental properties.

"In 1988," says Tracy, "we noticed a fourplex across the street from one of Dad's rental properties that had had a vacancy for quite a while, which told us that it wasn't being managed well. One day we saw a lady over there who didn't look like she lived there, so we went over and talked to her. It was the landlord.

The fourplex was located in Egg Harbor, about a 15-minute drive from the Fitzgerald's home in Absecon, New Jersey. Tracy and her father found out that the owner had bought the property for tax reasons when her husband passed away. A real estate management firm had been handling the fourplex, and not doing a very good job of it. The owner was very discouraged.

Says Tracy: "She hadn't really thought about selling it, but she didn't really want to keep it, either. So Dad and I talked and decided that we'd put a bid in for it."

It was also decided that Tracy—not her parents—would buy this property. It would be something to cut her teeth on in the business, and more importantly, it would represent the first step in her own program for financial freedom.

"When we approached the lady about buying her fourplex," Tracy recalls, "she said, 'There *is* a God! He has seen my problem and has sent me the solution.' So she was very happy. She would get a monthly income from selling it, yet she wouldn't have to worry about anything."

Negotiations Were Quick and Easy

The owner said she wanted $115,000, but would accept $110,000 with a $10,000 down payment. A $54,000 existing first mortgage would have to be assumed, with 12 remaining years of $715 monthly payments. This left a balance of $46,000, which the seller would carry back on a second mortgage loan.

After running the numbers, Tracy and Ed asked that this $46,000 mortgage loan be structured on a 12-year amortization schedule. The rental income would support the additional $408-per-month payments, and this way, both mortgages would be paid off in the same year—when Tracy would be 30 years old.

The only hitch was the $10,000 down payment. Not surprisingly, young Tracy didn't have it. But her parents did—or at least, they could get it. Anxious to see her get into the business, they got a bank loan and in turn loaned it to her. When the property sells, they will get the $10,000 back, plus 20 percent of the profits.

New Owner on the Block

The deal was consummated and Tracy became the only kid on the block to own four rental units. "It was exciting," she remembers, "because I felt like I was doing something great. But then all of a sudden it got scary. I mean, I didn't even have a checking account yet. Maybe balancing a checkbook isn't a big deal to some people, but it was to me.

"I had bills coming in, a vacancy to fill, and a tenant with a cat. I was really nervous showing the apartment because I had to show it to people who were a lot older than I was. It was intimidating. They'd ask if I could lower the rent, and I'd say, 'Well, maybe . . .' And I had to write a letter to the tenant with the cat telling him he had to get rid of it. I didn't feel that I should have that kind of power. But I did because I owned the building."

The fourplex was in good shape when Tracy bought it. Nevertheless, she had to make some repairs and improvements. But she cut the cost of these by doing whatever she could herself. Her year-and-a-half stint working for her father (actually, she had watched him work on apartments since she was seven years old) had made her quite capable of handling a broad spectrum of maintenance problems. When the water heater broke, for instance, she put on her work boots and took care of it herself . . . with a little help from her father, whom she claims can fix anything.

The four rental units brought in about $1,585 per month. With her $1,123 total mortgage payments and other operating expenses, she didn't have to put any money into monthly operating expenses, but then again, she wasn't getting any cash out of it. In short, it was a break-even cash flow situation.

Tracy admits that it took about a year and a half for her to realize the value of her investment. "I kept thinking that it was a big drain for me because I put a lot of time into it, yet I wasn't seeing cash pile up in my new bank account," she explains. "Here I was spending my days off mowing the lawn, putting in new window panes, doing the paperwork, and I didn't have $50 to go to the mall.

"Finally I grasped the concept that I *was* getting it back—and more—because the property was appreciating, and the tenants were paying off my mortgages. Now I realize how much money I was *really* making."

Her parents are living proof of the value of real estate investments. "My Dad and Mom own four apartment buildings with 38 rental units," says Tracy. "They mapped out a 10-year plan that I've been watching. That's how I know that real estate works. They saved and saved. We didn't have *anything* in our old house. Everything went back into the properties.

"But it worked. And it didn't even take the full ten years. They built their dream house a year ago. It's absolutely beautiful. And he didn't get it by working at the fire house. So I know it works. My Mom handles the rents and the business end of it, and my Dad does all the fix-up work. I hope I'll have that sort of thing some day."

She is on her way to achieving that goal. At present, the fourplex she purchased in '88 for $110,00 is now worth about $135,000 (which is wonderful considering the general real estate climate in the area). The property's monthly rental income is now $1,705, so she's getting a small positive monthly cash flow—a benefit that will increase as rents climb.

Tracy does what she can to keep expenses down. For instance, she went before the tax commission to appeal the fourplex's property taxes, which she considered to be too high. The commission agreed and they were lowered.

She has to spend very little time now managing the property. This allows her to maintain a full-time job without burning out. (She deals craps and blackjack in Atlantic City's Taj Mahal, making her an employee of another real estate entrepreneur—Donald Trump.)

"I had to paint an apartment a while ago," she explains, "but on a month-to-month basis, I really hardly ever have to do anything. I have good tenants, which my Mom says is the key."

Thirty Something

The real payoff will come in the year 2000. Tracy will be 30 then, and the mortgages will be paid off. That means that she can put the $1,123 that she's now paying in monthly mortgage payment into her own pocket, checking account, or perhaps into another property. And because rents will surely be much higher then than they are now, she'll have a much bigger positive monthly cash flow streaming in.

Not a bad situation to look forward to at the age of 30!

Does Tracy plan to keep the property? Absolutely. In fact, she's going to buy more rental real estate, which she also plans to hold and manage. "Our motto around here," she states, "is *'The day you sell real estate is the day you stop making money on it.'* "

Computerized Profits

In an era in which almost everything has become computerized, it could have been expected that rental property investing would also fall under the electronic net of the Information Age.

Dick Pranger, real estate investor from New Era, Michigan, confirms this. "I give my computer the credit for my best deal," he states. "It wouldn't have happened without it."

The saga begins in September of 1988. Dick had his eye on a six-unit property in the historic district of the nearby county seat of Hart, Michigan. It consisted of a large, wood-frame Victorian house with four rental units, plus a carriage house that had been divided up into two rental units. The 6,000-square-foot property had been brought to his attention by a real estate agent whom Dick had previously asked to keep his eye out for potential rental property buys.

"When the agent brought me the figures on the property," recalls Dick, "I ran them on my computer, using the **Financial Freedom Report's** MacFreedom™ real estate investor's software. I kept running numbers back and forth, back and forth. I didn't have very much cash, so I was trying to work something where I could get into it with as little down as possible. In order to do that, I had to get the price down, too."

The sellers were originally asking $89,000 for the six-unit property. Dick used the analysis module of the software to quickly determine the purchase price that the rental income would support. "The $89,000 suddenly dropped drastically," he says. "The computer told me that $89,000 was too high, but that a $60,000 purchase price would represent a real good deal for me. I could pay more than that, and still come out fine, but that was the price I should at least try to make work."

A Refusal He Wouldn't Take

In September, Dick offered $60,000—70 percent of which he would get from a bank loan and would give the seller in cash; 30 percent of which he would ask the seller to finance in the form of a 20-year second-mortgage loan, subordinate to the larger bank mortgage loan.

The sellers refused this offer.

Dick went back to his electronic drawing board, and in October, submitted offer number two, which the computer said would still be a good deal for him. The offer was for $75,000, with a $20,000 cash down payment, which Dick would get in the form of a bank loan. The sellers would take back a $45,000 mortgage, which they would have to subordinate to the $20,000 bank mortgage. The remaining $10,000 would be a trade. Dick would give the seller his motor home, valued at $10,000, as an additional part of the down payment.

Did the sellers want a trailer home? "I had no idea," laughs Dick. "I'm learning not to care too much about what sellers think. I have gotten into trouble trying to anticipate what other people are going to think. You have to do that to a certain extent, of course. You have to try to outguess them a little bit so you know what to do. But sometimes I would outguess *myself*. I'd assume that they wouldn't do this or wouldn't do that, when they really *would* have."

The sellers declined Dick's second offer. Back to the computer.

The third offer emerged three weeks later. This offer proposed a total price of $72,500 ($2,500 less than the previous offer). Of that amount, $3,500 would go to pay part of the sales commission, and would be in the form of a note to the real estate company, payable in six months. The sellers would pay the rest of the sales commission. Dick would get a first-mortgage loan from the bank for $41,500 and give that to the sellers in cash as a down payment. The sellers would carry back a $27,500 second-mortgage loan.

At that point, the sellers went to Florida for the winter.

"We had some conversations on the phone, and exchanged a few letters," recalls Dick, "but I could see we weren't going to accomplish much that way. We were having a hard enough time striking a deal in person."

Buying Some Time

In April of '89, the sellers were back and Dick and his computer had offer number four ready for them. In its fourth incarnation, the offer proposed a sales price of $73,500. Dick would personally come up with a $9,500 cash down payment, of which $6,000 would go to the sellers and $3,500 would go to the real estate company to help pay the commission. For the balance of $64,000, Dick would sign a straight land contract (called *contract for deed* in many areas of the country). This contract would be a 90-day contract with a 9½ percent interest rate, payable at $600 a month. At the end of the 90-day period, Dick would give the sellers an additional $24,000 cash, which he would borrow from a bank in the form of a first-mortgage loan. The sellers would carry back the $40,000 approximate balance on a 9½ percent interest second-mortgage loan (subordinated to the bank mortgage), which Dick would pay off with $375-per-month payments for five years, at which time the balance would be due and payable.

"The reason I did it this way was to give myself time," admits Dick. "I had indications that there might be someone else coming in to make an offer. So I wanted to lock the deal up with something the sellers would be happy with, and with something that would give me three months to get financing lined up."

Dick's persistence and creativity in designing offers paid off: the sellers accepted his fourth offer in April, 1989.

The property was already in good physical shape, with renters in all six units. The monthly income from rents was just under $1,170.

Dick got the loan within the 90-day time limit. But instead of borrowing $24,000, he was able to borrow $30,000. After giving the sellers their promised $24,000, he had $6,000 left over to replace most of the $9,500 cash he had put into the deal.

Dividing Four into Five

That fall, Dick maximized the income potential of the four-unit main house by turning it into a five-unit house. This gave him seven rentable units on the property. He spent about $8,500 to convert the attic into a fifth apartment. He did a third of the work himself and hired the rest done.

In the spring of 1990, the city of Hart offered a rental rehabilitation program for properties like Dick's. The city would pay half of all the approved rehab costs. Dick took advantage of it to put a new roof on the property, do new suspended ceilings, and add some facia, eaves, and other improvements. In all, Dick pumped $15,000 of improvements into the property, of which the city paid $7,500.

"What I didn't realize would happen when I got into this program," explains Dick, "is that because I had taken advantage of it, it put my property on the top of the list for Section Eight rental assistance program participants. And in this area of the country, there are long waiting lists of people trying to get into Section Eight housing.

"I got two or three existing tenants into the Section Eight program, and then I got a couple more Section Eight tenants after that. So I had about five of my units rented to people in the Section Eight program. By doing that, my rents actually increased."

In fact, because of the rental increases and the new attic apartment, the rental income rose to a little under $1,800 a month throughout 1990—over $600 a month more than what it was when Dick first assumed ownership.

In April of '91, the plot again thickened. Dick went to a bank and refinanced the property. The bank appraised the property for $117,500 (*$44,000 more than what Dick had paid for the property two years earlier*) and gave him a $70,000 first-mortgage loan, with which he paid off the original first-mortgage note of $30,000 (minus the principal he had paid down with the monthly payments).

He left the seller's existing second mortgage in place. It's principal balance had by then been reduced from its original $40,000 to roughly $38,000. "When I bought the property," Dick points out, "I stipulated in the contract that the mortgage note the sellers took back would be subordinated to any first position mortgage note I borrowed throughout the term of the contract. So if I refinanced at a future date, I could put the refinance lender in the first position ahead of their note, as I had done on the first $30,000 mortgage loan.''

Which is exactly what he did.

The property now has two mortgages against it: one for $70,000, the other for $3,800. The monthly payments on these mortgages are $795 and $375 respectively. With the increased rental income, this leaves Dick with a positive cash flow of about $300 per month after deducting all long- and short-term expenses, variable costs, and contingencies. Again, he used his computer program to help him determine and compute all these potential costs so he wouldn't be left short.

The "profits" from the refinancing loan must not be forgotten. Remember, the loan was for $70,000, and Dick only paid off the first mortgage, which was less than $30,000. After paying loan costs, that left Dick with over $40,000 in cash. This amount reimbursed him for the portion of the $8,500 and $7,500 improvement costs that had not already come back to him in the form of cash flow, and still left him with a sizable bundle, which, like the true investor he is, he pumped into other real estate investments.

Maintaining a Healthy Cash Flow

Dick gives much of the credit for the success of this deal to Mac-Freedom™, which enabled him to design, calculate, and know exactly where he stood with each of his four offers and the refinancing loan. Because of this, he has been able to achieve optimal financing while maintaining a healthy cash flow.

Dick's management skills (which also benefit from Mac-Freedom™, which includes a full management module), plus his foresight in converting the attic of the main house into a seventh apartment, were also key factors in the success of this investment.

"All in all," he concludes, "everything added up made this what I would have to call an extremely good deal."

CHAPTER 25

A Street-Smart Investment

Kenneth Hayes is a professional flipper. No, he is not with the circus. Nor is he a member of a traveling gymnastics team. It's not his body that he flips for a living—it's real estate . . . single-family homes to be exact. And he has flipped (bought, fixed up, and quickly resold) over 100 single-family homes worth in excess of $12 million in the past six years.

"My business is to purchase single-family homes in a two-day period," explains Kenneth. "I have a network set up that enables me to analyze a property in about six hours, cash out the seller in two days or less, fix it up, then turn around and sell it quickly. I don't stray from this type of investment. That's all I do. That's all I know."

Bread and Butter Deals

In October of 1990, Kenneth, who lives in Riverside, California (the Los Angeles area), received a call in response to one of the ads he continuously runs in three major Los Angeles area newspapers. The ads, which cost about $18,000 a year and are responsible for an average of 22 flipper properties annually, proclaim that he pays cash for homes within two days.

This particular call was from a woman who owned a home in a "bread and butter" neighborhood in the lower section of Santa Ana. The neighborhood was plagued by gang activity and violence.

The woman was a motivated seller. Her twelve-year-old son had been killed on the front lawn the year before in a drive-by shooting. After the tragedy, she moved away and rented the home out. Now, after dealing with abusive tenants for a year, she wanted out altogether and needed to be cashed out of the home in order to buy another residence.

During their phone conversation, Kenneth took out a prospectus sheet and asked the questions he always asks a potential seller. Then he set his "machine" in motion on the project by turning the prospectus sheet over to his researcher.

He explains: "The researcher is responsible for gathering all the data on the property, plus sales 'comps,' which she gets through the computer. Then she hands everything back to me. The whole process is done within a six-hour period.

"When the report hit my desk, I knew the property had real potential."

Fear of a Different Kind

Kenneth arranged to meet the seller at her house the following day. "Was I afraid to go down into that area?" he asks. "Yes, I was afraid, but I weighed the risks and I could see that this deal was worth it."

Armed with the knowledge the research report gave him, after seeing the property and talking with the owner, Kenneth offered her $94,200. She had been asking close to $115,000, but Kenneth explained that the reason he can cash people out in two days or less is because he purchases their homes for roughly 70 percent of their "as is" values. That's the way he does business, he told her.

In fact, he *never* pays more than 75 percent of a home's value. His other rule of thumb for his flipper investments is that he needs to net a minimum of $20,000 per property, or a minimum of 100 percent of the money he invests in a deal, whichever is higher.

The woman accepted the offer, and Kenneth bought the home on October 12, 1990. "She got a very good deal out of it," he says. "I assumed her first mortgage of $15,529, and gave her $78,671 in cash for the balance. With that she was able to go out and buy another home."

The $78,671 cash came from a quick $68,000 bank loan and Kenneth's own funds. "I have built up a rapport with a local bank," he explains. "If you're going to be a professional flipper, one of the keys to success is to have access to cash, and to be able to get it quickly. That's why I established a relationship with a local community bank five years ago, rather than with a major bank. Since then, I have gone to this bank for somewhere between 45 and 50 home purchases totaling about $6 millon.

"With that type of relationship and cooperation with a small community bank, you become a large fish in a small tank and you're allowed to do things that you wouldn't be able to do in a large bank. For instance, you can shorten the loan process so that you can move quickly on deals. In the bigger banks, where loan requests have to go through committees and whatnot, it takes forever.

"At my local community bank, with my track record with them, I can get loans in two or three days. If there's really a rush, they can actually prepare documents and get me a check within four hours. By having that type of cooperation, it gives me the flexibility to maintain control over transactions and beat the competition.

"When I went into this business, my thinking was to establish myself as a money person—a cash buyer—to the sellers out there, and create a system that would enable me to close deals in three days or less. By doing that, my services would definitely be worthy of motivated sellers."

The Right Agent for the Right People

Kenneth decided that another critical key to the success of this project would be to find an aggressive Spanish-speaking real estate agent who wouldn't be afraid of the area and could provide him with a buyer. Even before he went over to look at the house the first time, he found what he was looking for in the person of a $13-million-a-year real estate agent who found two buyers for the house even before he had closed on the purchase of the home. In fact, this agent accompanied him on his first visit to the property.

"Although it looked like a pigsty at the time," he explains, "I was able to tell her how much money would be allocated toward the fix-up cost, and how I was going to 'cherry out' the property. This gave her the confidence to sell it to her buyers before I even purchased it. She was able to go through her network of Hispanic buyers and find the right people."

Kenneth had predetermined that he would renovate the home and sell it for about $151,000. "Believe it or not," he says, "$150,000 is the lower-priced property in Orange County. You can't buy a piece of junk for less than $150,000. This particular home was a typical three-bedroom, 1¾ bathroom, 1,200 square-foot home that needed a cosmetic facelift. We knew that when we were finished it would be the kind of home the neighborhood would be proud of. Other homes were for sale in the neighborhood—homes that weren't as nice as this was going to be—and all of them were priced higher than the $151,000 that we would be asking."

Money Talks

Before he could proceed with his plans for the house, however, Kenneth had to get the existing tenants out. To do this, he had his Spanish-speaking real estate agent go talk to them (they spoke Spanish) and offer them $500 to move somewhere else. One hundred dollars would be paid up-front and the remaining $400 would be theirs the moment they vacated the property and handed the agent the key.

The tenants were gone within two weeks.

"I believe in giving people money rather than fighting with them," explains Kenneth. "You should never go to court to evict tenants. Instead, you should pay them to get out. By paying the tenant, you avoid court time. If you're in the flip-and-sell business and you're paying debt service on property, it does you no good to sit there for three months waiting for a court date.

"This gets into the *street-smart approach*. If you're in business, you have to treat it like a business."

The next step was to "cherry-out" the property, as Kenneth refers to it. He ordered his crew to descend on the home and its yard and get to work.

"The fix-up costs on this property would have been $15,000," he points out. But because I have my own fix-up crew, I was able to get the job done for less. The six people on the crew painted the exterior and interior, remodeled the kitchen, cleaned up the yard, did light carpentry repairs, installed new carpeting and floor coverings, and thoroughly checked out the heating/air-conditioning systems. We have a step-by-step procedure, and we offer home warranty protection plans. The crew was in and out in ten days.

"What really helped us out on this one is the fact that my crew foreman is an Hispanic gentleman who speaks fluent Spanish. He was able to create a rapport with the neighbors so they would keep an eye out on the house and wouldn't tear it up.

"That's one of the street-smart techniques we use when we go into lower bread-and-butter areas. We become friends with the neighbors and even pay them to watch the property. We'll pay one or two neighbors $50 to $75 a month to keep their eyes on the house and let us know immediately if anyone tries to vandalize it."

As stated earlier, Kenneth's real estate agent had found two buyers even before she and Kenneth went to look at the home. Seventeen days after Kenneth purchased the home for $94,200, one of these buyers signed a sales agreement to buy the house for $151,000. The buyer made a $2,000 nonrefundable deposit and the deal went into escrow on October 29, 1990, with a 30-day closing deadline. The closing took place on the 11th of November—23 days later.

What did Kenneth do with the $151,000 check he received at the closing? First, the $68,000 and the $15,529 mortgages had to be paid off. This left him with $67,471. From this, he paid back the extra money he personally put into the purchase, plus fix-up expenses, closing costs and all other expenses, including sales commissions.

Polishing the Diamond

After everything was paid, Kenneth walked away with a *net profit of $30,800.*

"Looking back," says Kenneth, "I realize that what made this deal so interesting and successful was that I had the foresight and the guts to walk into a difficult situation and make it work—to take a diamond in the rough and make it shine. Where other investors wouldn't touch a property like that with a ten-foot pole, I saw extreme opportunity in it.

"What made it all come together so well was having my rehab people get in and do the job quickly, getting the right real estate agent to work with the existing tenants and find a cash buyer, and getting into and out of the deal in only 40 days. That's from the day I bought it to the day I sold it. I didn't even have to make a payment on the loans."

During the short duration of the project, Kenneth didn't have to spend very much of his own time on it. "I personally spent a grand total of 2½ hours on this property," he says, "including the 40-minute drive time from Riverside to Santa Ana. I went down to see the property twice—the day I went to look at it with the woman who was selling it, and the day I sold it."

For just a handful of hours of personal involvement, $30,800 represents an excellent per-hour wage.

Of course, it must be admitted that such successes could not have materialized without years of effort in building a razor-sharp flipper system. "It's a system that is responsible for flipping anywhere from 21 to 27 single-family homes a year," asserts Kenneth. "This year I'm doing better than ever before, even though it's a recessionary market. I'm on my way to doing $5 million retail in single-family home flippers."

CHAPTER 26

Making Beautiful Music in Real Estate

John Bayer is a high school music teacher who makes beautiful financial music on the side by investing in income-producing real estate.

Early in 1989, he and his wife, Sylvia, (who is his working partner in their real estate business) heard about a three-unit apartment property in the small rural village of Perry, New York, just eight miles away from their home in the similarly small (4,000 population) village of Warsaw.

The Victorian-style property was comprised of three residential flats, one on top of the other. It was located on the main street running through town. Overall, the building was in good shape. A recent tax assessment had placed the property's value at $60,000, and the seller was asking $59,900. The rents at that time were $275, $230, and $230—on the low side for the area and the property.

"I asked the real estate agent if the seller would be willing to carry a second mortgage if I came in with a first mortgage," says John. "The agent said he thought he'd be willing to carry some paper, since he'd been trying to sell the property for over six months. He also indicated that he had two other appointments to show the property. He said somebody was quite interested. Now, I didn't know whether he was just trying to get me to move faster or what, but he'd been straight with me in the past, so I had no reason not to believe him. Besides, I had the advantage of being able to run the numbers on the property quickly on my computer.''

A Byte of Technology

That night, John went home and generated an analysis of the property on his computer using the **Financial Freedom Report's** Mac-Freedom™ software. The next day he called the agent and said he was ready to make an offer.

Says John: ''I wrote an offer that said I would go to the bank and get a first mortgage for $45,000, if he would be willing to hold a second mortgage for $15,000. It also said that the purchase price would be $57,000.

The real estate agent wasn't used to this sort of addition. He pointed out that $45,000 and $15,000 didn't equal $57,000. ''I know that,'' said John. ''They add up to $60,000.''

The agent scratched his head.

''It's okay,'' John assured him, ''as long as nobody has any hang-ups with it. There's nothing wrong with this as long as the property appraises high enough to cover both mortgages.''

So it was written into the offer that it was contingent on the bank appraising the property for a minimum of $60,000. (The appraisal actually came in at $62,000.)

The offer and a $550 deposit were accepted in mid May, '89, after a little negotiating. John had asked for a six-month moratorium on the second mortgage, during which time no payment would have to be made and no interest would accrue. The seller didn't like this, and offered to drop the 10½ percent interest rate he had planned to charge to 10 percent if John would forget the moratorium. John agreed.

So it was settled that the seller's mortgage note would carry 10 percent interest, that it would be amortized over 30 years, starting immediately upon purchase, and that the interest rate would be renegotiated at the end of five years. The payments on this mortgage would be $131 per month.

Different Colored Horses

The $45,000 first mortgage, however, was a horse of a different color. John explains: "The only commercial loans we have around here are one-year, renegotiated interest loans. So they really socked it to us with a 13½ percent interest rate that first year. But it's now down to 12½ percent and will drop to about 11 percent soon. The loan is amortized over 20 years. The payments were set at $535 per month. Even though the interest rate has come down, they keep the payment the same and just apply more to the principal pay-down, which is fine because we build up equity quicker that way."

As it happened, both John and the seller had the same attorney. He agreed to represent both parties and lower the closing costs. And he had no problems with John borrowing $60,000 for a $57,000 purchase.

"It was interesting," John remarks, "that our banker didn't mind the fact that we weren't putting any of our own money into the purchase. And it didn't bother him that there was a second mortgage on the home worth $3,000 more than what we needed to make the purchase. These things didn't bother him because of the professional, organized presentation—the one I generated using MacFreedom™.

"It's obvious you're not putting any of your own money into this," said the banker. "But I can see that you know to such great detail what this building's going to do, that I don't think we'll have any problem. If you had come in here with just a piece of paper and a calculator, we might have had a problem."

According to John: "It's important to have that professional look, to know your numbers, your plans, your contingencies. It makes a big difference."

John closed the purchase of the three-unit property at the end of June, 1989. Because he had financed it for $3,000 more than the sales price, he walked away with $2,198 after paying closing costs. Of course, $500 of that went to pay him back for the deposit he had made with the offer. This still left him with a nice $1,698 "profit" on a deal in which he had put none of his own money.

He didn't use the $1,698 to take Sylvia to the Bahamas, however. Instead, he plowed it back into the property in the form of improvements, including painting, almost all of which he hired out. In fact, he had a contractor go over the building from top to bottom to make sure everything was in good shape—from the roof to the baseboards.

All in all, he put $3,250 into improvements during the first eight months of ownership. However, he only had to come up with $1,552 of that amount personally, thanks to the $1,698 he received at the closing.

Inching Up the Rents

The property generated a slight negative cash flow for a little less than a year. The rental income totaled $735 per month, which was a little less than the $666 total monthly mortgage payments plus other operating expenses. "But I knew that up front," adds John. "The computer told us exactly what the building was going to do and that's what it did. It helped to know ahead of time what we could expect."

As forecast, the negative cash flow soon turned into a break-even and sometimes slightly positive situation in June of 1991 as John inched up the rents. "I'm raising rents on a very gradual basis," he points out, "so that I don't shock my tenants. I have some very good renters in there—some nice, professional people—and it's working out nicely. My plan is to continue raising rents a bit every six months until I get them up to where they should be."

Currently, the rents are $275, $290, and $310, and the tenants pay all utilities. The coming rent increase will raise them to $285, $310, and $335, for a total of $930. "That will put us well into a positive cash flow situation," says John. "We'll have one more increase six months after that to get them to market levels. After that, we'll have regular annual increases.

"The property is pretty much on 'auto pilot' at this point. It's in good shape. My plumber and electrician are always on call. They scoot right over whenever there's a problem. I just go over there every ten days to make sure that things are tidy, that the back hall is swept, and that the light bulbs haven't burned out. And it's easy for me to visit because it's on my way to work."

Bought Smart

The Bayers are planning to keep the property. Why not? It's a breeze to manage, the positive cash flow will grow each year, and their equity grows each time a tenant pays rent.

In addition, this tidy, well-managed, three-unit building is appreciating in value faster than what is normal for the area and the type of property. "Yesterday, a real estate broker told me it could market easily at $75,000," claims John.

That's $18,000 worth of equity in less than two years—forced equity that John and Sylvia have earned by buying smart, fixing up, and managing properly. When this equity—which will grow over the years—is combined with the positive cash flow that they'll be receiving, it becomes obvious that the $2,500 or so of their own money that they have put into the project (in improvements and to cover early negative cash flow) has indeed been well spent.

CHAPTER 27

The Nest That Became a Nest Egg

As real estate investors go, Nick Anagnostis is relatively conservative. This is not surprising. In fact, given what he went through as a child, it is surprising that he had the courage to jump into the rental property business at all.

During the most impressionable years of his youth, Nick saw his family torn away from its home—a home that his father had built and paid for with $2,500 cash. His parents hadn't known that the land the home sat on had been mortgaged, and when the payment came due, the bank foreclosed and took it back . . . house and all. This was during the Great Depression.

The event left a deep impression on young Nick.

Nevertheless, almost three decades later, Nick realized that if he ever wanted to give himself, his wife, and his family long-term financial security, he had to do more than depend on his earnings as an American Airlines employee.

"The only way that I could see that I'd make any money," recalls Nick, "would be to buy a piece of property, rent it out, and let the tenants pay off the mortgage. So despite my childhood experiences, which told me never to risk anything, I bought my first little rental home in 1960, and three more in '62."

Deep in the Heart of Texas

His best deal was one of these 1962 acquisitions.

The property was located in a nice, though aging neighborhood on the west side of Fort Worth, Texas, not far from his home in the community called Euless.

It was a 1½ story house badly in need of repair, and he bought it from an older couple for $5,500, paying $500 down and putting the $5,000 balance on a 12-year, 6 percent interest mortgage note. The payments were less than $50 a month.

"The only problem was that I didn't have the money to make repairs," says Nick. "So, having heard about FHA, I decided to go to my friendly banker who had loaned me $50 once. I said, 'I need some money. What about an FHA home improvement loan?' And he said, 'Sure, we make all kinds of those loans.'

"He told me I'd need a contractor and a list of improvements to be done, and the approximate costs. I got a friend of mine to be the contractor, and they gave me a $2,500, three-year loan. So we put on a new roof and repaired the insides. I bought 180 sheets of sheet rock for that house at $1.50 a sheet. I was working hard at American Airlines so I didn't have time to actually do the work myself. But I bought all the materials and got the right people to do the work."

To make a long story short, Nick got the house in good shape and rented it out. "Not only did I get it in A-1 condition," he says, "but I had some money left over when I was finished to put in my pocket: the *Hip* National Bank."

A Laughing Banker

The $2,500 FHA loan didn't turn out to be the low-interest bonanza Nick had assumed it would be. "By the time I got through paying it," he quips, "I found out that FHA didn't mean low interest rates—FHA meant whatever the bank wanted to charge, and FHA insured it. If I remember correctly, they charged me about 12 percent back then. When I was getting ready to pay it off, I told my banker, 'What the devil is this? I didn't realize I owed that much! I thought this was an FHA loan!'

"He said, 'Sure it is. It was *insured* by FHA, but we charge whatever we can charge. That's the way we make our money!' And he was laughing!"

That was the way Nick learned a lot of his lessons in the real estate business, he points out.

The renovated home stayed rented for the next eight years. While Nick's equity in the property grew during that time as his tenants' payments paid down the mortgage and paid off the small FHA loan, he wasn't seeing much in the way of cash flow. Admitting that he didn't have much of a bookkeeping system back then, and can't point to exact cash flow figures, he recalls that it was just slightly above break even.

By 1970 he was tired of this property and wanted out. A recent promotion had made him facility manager of the American Airlines buildings in his area, increasing his work load, his pay, and his pension. Besides, he owned other rental properties at this time, so why hang onto a little house that wasn't giving him a good monthly cash flow?

Nick decided to sell, but an interested person wanted to lease the home rather than buy it. "I'd never leased anything," he states. "It just wasn't customary around here. But I went ahead and leased it for 12 months, and got a pretty decent cash flow out of it. It was a good deal as far as I was concerned. The second year came up and this family begged me to let them lease it another year. So I raised the lease a bit, made them agree to send me a check each month and take care of any minor repairs, and signed them up for another year."

To make another long story short, this relationship lasted for thirteen years. Says Nick: "I raised the lease a few times and was making a very good cash flow. And I never had to paint it, plunge a toilet, fix a leaky faucet . . . I didn't have to *touch* that property while those people were in it. The water heater went out one year, so I told them to go out and buy one on their charge card, install it themselves, and deduct the cost from their rent."

Time Marches On

By 1984—a year after Nick had retired from his American Airlines job—some of the houses in the area in which the leased home was located were being torn down and new townhouses were being built in their places. A real estate agent called Nick that year, saying that he had a client who might be interested in buying his home.

"Sir, there's no sign out there," said Nick. "You know that I don't want to sell the property."

"Well, *would* you sell the house?" responded the agent.

"Sir, I'd sell anything I have except my wife." Nick admits that he was enjoying having the upper hand, since he wasn't motivated to sell.

"What would you take for it?" queried the agent.

"Look," said Nick, "you're the one who's proposing something here. If you've got a client who wants the house, write up a contract, bring me an escrow check, and then we'll talk about it. But I'll tell you right now, I wouldn't take a penny less than $100,000 for it."

This was positive thinking on Nick's part. He knew that the property was worth a minimum of $50,000 at that time. But he also knew that the agent calling him was from a commercial brokerage house. As a commercial property, the land would be worth more than it would be as a residential house and lot. He knew $100,000 would be high, but he also knew that it would get the agent and buyer thinking in the right direction.

It must also be kept in mind that the property had been paid off years ago, and Nick was getting over $200 a month in rents with the tenant handling all maintenance and paying all costs except a small annual tax and insurance bill.

Within 24 hours, the agent called Nick, announcing that he had a written offer and deposit. He said he'd bring it to Nick's house, but Nick said he had to bring his car to a shop near the agent's office, so he'd meet him there.

The office was luxurious. They sat down at the conference table, a secretary brought Nick some coffee, and they exchanged some small talk. "Sir," said Nick after a few minutes, "I don't want to be discourteous, but I've got to get my car into the shop. Do you have something to talk about?"

Offers and Counteroffers

He did. It was a contract to buy the home for $80,000 cash, with a 6 percent sales commission that Nick would have to pay. Nick folded up the contract, said he'd think about it, thanked them for the coffee, and left.

That night, Nick crossed out the $80,000 and wrote in *$85,000*, then crossed out the 6 percent commission, and wrote in *3 percent*. He reduced the commission because he himself had been a real estate agent since '75, and he knew that any broker is going to expect to co-broker a deal. So he would save $2,550 by keeping half the proposed commission.

Nick took the revised offer back the following day. The agent didn't say a word about the $85,000 counteroffer, but balked at the reduced commission. When Nick explained his reasoning, the agent conceded to it stoically.

The buyer accepted, initialled the changes, and the deal was on.

"If he hadn't accepted the $85,000," says Nick, "I would have taken $80,000. The house had been paid for by the tenants' payments for many years, and I'd made many thousands of dollars on cash flow."

That's not the end of the story, however.

Nick asked his accountant what the $85,000 cash would do to his tax liability that year. The accountant ran a few numbers, shook his head, and said it didn't look good.

"What if I took $40,000 of it this year, and the other $45,000 of it on January 2 next year?" asked Nick.

That would save Nick about $9,000, his accountant told him. So Nick asked the real estate agent if the buyer would agree to pay him $40,000 at closing and the other $45,000 on January 2. (He knew that if he had the money into a certificate of deposit by the third day of the month, he'd get interest for that month.) The agent called back the following day and said the buyer would be happy to do that, and pay 10 percent interest.

The Retiring Life

Nick hadn't thought of that! In addition to saving $9,000 in taxes, this maneuver would bring him over $1,000 in interest (about three months' worth).

In fact, interest was what interested Nick. His plan was to put all $85,000 into a secure, interest-bearing savings instrument, leave the principal alone, and draw off the interest whenever he needed it. That's exactly what he did, and continues to do.

"That was the deal that put me on the top shelf and secured my retirement," claims Nick. "I have a retirement plan from American Airlines, and of course my wife and I get Social Security, but that $85,000 in the bank is our money that we travel with and spend foolishly several times a year. I have other profits from some other real estate deals I've done in the bank, too, plus income from properties that are still producing. So our retirement is made."

Nick concludes: "I knew years ago that as a poor man who had to work for a living, the only way I was going to get ahead was by investing in real estate. I tried stock. It didn't bring me anything. I bought some rental properties, and they've been making me tons of money from the first day I rented them."

CHAPTER 28

The Original Animal House

G eorge Rohmeyer's best deal involves a 17-unit "animal house."

The saga began for this Marshfield, Wisconsin real estate entrepreneur in 1986. The apartment building had been for sale for about four years. The owners had originally been asking $400,000, but had softened on their price over the years.

Why hadn't the property sold? "It's located next to the University of Wisconsin here in town," explains George, "and students rent it. In fact, it's the only large building that is there for student housing. Other students are scattered all over town. There are seventeen apartments, but each apartment holds four students, so there were about 68 students in it. It was pretty torn up, to say the least. It was an animal house."

But the poor condition of the building was not its only flaw. The man who had orginally built the apartment property was the owner of a construction company. He built the building and a few others like it on other campuses in an effort to develop an "in" with the state, with the objective of getting major construction contracts for university buildings.

His arrangement with the University for these student housing buildings was interesting. The state government, or universities, put up the land and all improvements. The contractor built the buildings. After 40 years, the contractor would deed the buildings to the university. During that 40 years, he would get whatever cash flow the apartments generated.

That was the deal. The particular building that was for sale, in which George was interested, had 26 years remaining before it had to be deeded to the university. And, as already mentioned, it was in bad shape.

Hard Players

The contractor died about five years before this time, leaving his two sons in charge of the construction company and its rental properties. Where the father had worked hard and drove trucks, the sons played hard and drove Jaguars. What the father had left them soon began coming apart at the seams, including this apartment property. The boys, unwilling to put the time and effort into managing it profitably, wanted out. They put it on the market not long after their father's death.

"I had known about this property since it went up for sale," says George, "But when I found out that it had to be deeded back to the university in the year 2011, I put it out of my mind. But in 1986 a friend of mine made an offer on the property for $150,000, subject to him being able to trade some second mortgage paper he owned for about $50,000 of that price. They accepted that.

"He got an appraisal on the property, which came in at $150,000, subject to about $30,000 or $40,000 in needed repairs. This scared him off. He backed out. That's when I got involved.

"Even though I live in a small community, there's quite a network of people I work with. If one guy smells out a deal and decides not to act on it, we'll give him $100, $500, $1,000, or whatever it's worth to take it over. My friend had paid $660 for the appraisal, so what I did was swap him this deal for another deal that I had been working on. My next step was to offer the owners $50,000 cash for the 17-unit property and all the beds, dressers, and furniture that came with it. I was looking for the bottom."

He almost found it. The contractor's sons countered with $95,000, with them holding a second mortgage for $20,000, and the remaining $75,000 to be paid in cash at closing. The $20,000, second mortgage would be amortized at 8 percent interest over 10 years.

"I accepted that," states George. "Normally I would have tried to beat them down another $5,000 to $10,000, but there was an underlying mortgage that had to be satisfied. Actually, the real reason I accepted it so quickly was that the vultures were circling. The whole thing was so sweet I wanted to close it up so I wouldn't lose it."

Not a Pretty Picture

The deal was struck in August of 1986. It closed on November 4, three months later. But a lot happened between the day they shook hands on the original agreement and the moment they walked out of the closing.

For one thing, he had to line up financing for the $75,000 cash payment. "When I took my banker through the building," recalls George, "I took him over on a Monday morning, which I thought would be a good time to go. There was a guy running around the hall in his underwear. Water was running out of the front of the building. A bunch of girls were having a water fight. Luckily, my banker knew that I knew what I was doing, and had enough confidence in me to approve the loan anyway."

George also had to prepare a management system that could be set in motion immediately upon taking over the property. Realizing that he needed to have someone on the premises to maintain control, he entered into an agreement with his unmarried, 27-year-old nephew, Danny Fink.

"I will take you on as a full 50-50 partner in this building for as long as we own it," George told him. "You don't have to put any money into it. All you have to do is live in the building and manage it." Not surprisingly, the nephew accepted.

George orchestrated the November 4 closing like a symphony. For starters, he made sure it took place in his attorney's office. He also had the $75,000 he had borrowed from his bank on a first mortgage in his attorney's trust account, ready to go. In addition, he had an estimate for $1,900 in repair costs to repair one of the building's two water heaters, plus an inventory of the broken furniture.

Before the closing, George planned out exactly what he was going to say and do, and told his lawyer, "I do not want you to say a thing. You're working for me. Just sit behind your desk and look stern."

The participants at the closing were George, his nephew Danny, his lawyer, the seller (one of the brothers), and the real estate agent. The closing proceeded, and soon the $20,000 seller-carried second mortgage was brought out for signing.

"Hold it," said George. "We have a little problem here that we're going to have to rectify. There's a leaky water heater and a lot of broken furniture in the building. When I offered to buy the property, I did so in good faith, and I assumed that everything was in reasonably good shape."

After a bit of hum-hawing, George said to the seller, "I understand your problem. You don't have the time to take care of these things. So what I'll do to make it less painful for you is this: I'll accept the leaky water heater and broken furniture if you'll knock $5,000 off that second mortgage."

George noticed that the seller visibly stiffened. "I need to call my controller," he said, getting up and leaving the room. When he returned a few minutes later, he muttered, "Take the - - - - - - - thing! Let's get this deal done."

So George bought the property for $90,000 instead of $95,000.

It Gets Better

The student tenants pay their rents a semester in advance. Even though the purchase closed on November 4, George had engineered the deal in advance so that the rents would be prorated as though he had purchased the property on September 1. *This made him the happy recipient of $28,000 in student rents at the closing!*

"So the seller had to give *me* a check for $28,000 for the prorated rents," explains George, "after having just lost $5,000 for the water heater and broken furniture."

After the closing, George took $10,000 of the dollars he carried away from the closing and immediately paid the $75,000 first mortage loan down to $65,000. He set aside $12,000 to put into repairs and improvemnts, and split the other $6,000 "pocket money" with Danny.

At this point, George had a $65,000 first mortgage and a $15,000 second mortgage on the property, with a $12,000 fund to spend for improvements—not to mention the $6,000 he and Danny carried away as spoils of real estate war.

His next step was to get Danny moved into the animal house. Then he raised the rents and went to work with his nephew to set in motion a cost-effective property management and improvement system.

For instance: "I went to a Holiday Inn," says George. "They were refurbishing, and I bought all of their carpet. It's a high quality, medium-brown carpet. We went all through our building, tore out all the junky carpet, and replaced it with this used carpet. Laid, I had about $2 a yard into it. And it's $20-a-yard stuff." After all was said and done, George and Danny put about $15,000 into improving the building.

They also went to work to cut costs. For example, a local company was hauling garbage from the building. The cost: over $500 a month. George fired them, built a trailer, parked it in the back, and had Danny haul garbage to the local landfill once a week for a total cost of $60 a month.

Because they were paying the heating costs, they bought and installed double-strength storm windows for the largest window openings in each apartment. These windows go on late in October and don't come off until the beginning of May. This keeps the students from leaving the large windows open during cold months and cranking up the heat. After the first year, the heating company did an audit and discovered that the building was using 40 percent less heating fuel thanks to this measure.

Growing a Cash Flow

Using such strategies, George and Danny were able to cut operating costs by 40 percent the first year. The building brought them $55,000 in gross rents. Their net profit, even after debt service, was about $22,000.

With their continued efforts the cash flow grew. Having kicked out about half the tenants he "inherited," George and Danny worked on getting better behaved renters and upgrading the overall image of the apartment building. By the end of two years, they had a 100 percent occupancy factor with a waiting list of students that wanted to move in.

During the three-month summer vacation when the building was usually vacant, George started renting out the apartments by the week to such tenants as management interns and people who were in between houses because of relocations. He promotes this short-term rental program through realty firms. This strategy alone has been bringing in *an additional $12,000 each summer, more or less.*

Within the first three years of ownership, George completely paid off the $65,000 first mortgage out of cash flow proceeds.

Because the $15,000 second mortgage was only 8 percent interest, there was little incentive to pay it off early. However, the brothers who sold George the property had gone through a bankruptcy shortly after the closing, and now that the dust has settled, George is negotiating with them to make a cash payment of $3,000 to buy out the mortgage. The principal balance is now approximately $10,000. George claims that he normally pays between 30 and 50 cents on the dollar to cash out a mortgage note, but adds that the 8 percent interest rate puts time on his side.

Harvesting Profit

Based on current revenues, the 17-unit property will pull in between $80,000 and $90,000 in gross income this year, with a net profit of approximately $50,000. George is using much of his half of those profits to accelerate the payoffs of the mortgages on the other hundred or so apartments he owns. In short, the property is a money-machine.

This is not the end of the story.

What about the deed provision that says George has to give the property back to the University in the year 2011? No problem according to George. He has found out that the University does not want to own and manage the building, and is sure that it will be willing to let him buy it out.

But what is really exciting to George is this: in the contract, he is given the right to build up to three additional 17-unit apartment buildings on the same plot of ground any time until the year 2011, and run them for 40 years. "The University just expanded," he points out. "Plus, they just fiished construction on a brand new technical school right next to our property. And like I said before, *our building is the only game in town!*

"When I tell people about this deal, they say 'Well, *I* couldn't do that.' That's not true. Anybody can do these types of deals. But they've got to do their homework. And they've got to be willing to stick with it and not give up. Instead of being turned off and not pursuing a potential deal, they've got to keep turning over stones."

George laughs, "I could retire off this one project. Now, because I've got my nephew in there as an on-site partner, I don't even have to look at the property. I sit down once a month with him and pay bills. That's it.

"But you have to keep in mind that I've been doing this kind of thing since 1977. If I hadn't done a lot of other projects, I wouldn't have been able to see my way clear to make this deal."

An RTC Success Story

At a time when real estate investors from coast to coast were complaining that their efforts to buy RTC properties had resulted only in frustration, one Midwest investor proved that it could be done, and done profitably.

"I read an article that was very negative about working with the RTC," says Candace Balfour-Broecker of Batavia, Illinois (near Chicago). "But I didn't find this to be the case. I had an exceedingly good experience with the RTC, and with the RTC contact I dealt with here in Chicago.

"I had to be persistent, though, because there were some subtle nuances in this deal that had to be pursued. It took some time, and yes, we experienced some frustration at first because all of our questions couldn't be answered immediately. But I persisted, and they were willing to get the information and sit down and explain things to us."

A True Gem

In 1990 Candace had seen an article in a Chicago newspaper about a 19-unit apartment property that the RTC was selling. The article raved about the historic register building, and claimed that it was one of the true gems in the RTC inventory.

The property consisted of four and a half acres of land, on which sat a main building with 14 residential apartments, plus five more townhouse units. It was located in a neighborhood of very nice residences whose average value was about $200,000, and was originally a school built in 1855. During one period in the 1970s, it was virtually abandoned and in disrepair.

In the early 1980s a limited partnership bought the property and put about $2 million dollars into rehabilitating it into condominiums and adding five new townhouses. But the partnership ran out of funds before it could add the "sizzle," such as the landscaping and detail work that can make or break a project.

In 1985, the property was sold to a new owner for $1,780,000, which was considered a steal. Then came the Tax Reform Act of 1986, which contributed to the new owner's inability to keep up mortgage payments. To make a painful story short, the savings and loan that held the mortgage had to foreclose on the property and take it back. Then the S&L itself went bad, and the RTC became the owner of the property.

It was after the RTC had owned the property for about a year that Candace arranged to take a look at it. At that time, rumors were flying around that the place was in shambles and that it was definitely a bad risk.

"The property got a bad reputation," says Candace. "That's when I got interested. Some of my best deals have been properties with bad reputations. To me, it spells *opportunity.,*"

On January 6, 1991, Candace, together with her husband (Howard), her partners, her real estate agent, and the real estate agent hired by the RTC to sell the propety met to walk through it.

"By the time we had seen three of the apartments," Candace recalls, "I turned to my real estate agent and said, 'Alex, get out a contract!' It was nothing like they said it would be. Thirteen of the sixteen apartments were rented. The structure was absolutely beautiful, and in quite good condition. It had a marble entry hall, beautiful exterior, and so on.

"The property had been appraised and an estimate of repairs had been made. The repair estimate turned out to be considerably higher than what was necessary. When I got my own contractor in there, he gave me a repair estimate that came to only $25,000."

Making the Offer

The RTC was asking $650,000 for the property, having reduced the price within just the past month. This was during the Gulf War crises—one of the softest times for real estate in recent history. The $650,000 was considerably less than what the property sold for in '85, and substantially less than an appraisal Candace had obtained.

Candace, Howard, and their partners decided to offer $550,000 cash, with a $25,000 earnest money deposit (each of the two partner couples chipped in $12,500). She would also specify a 28-day inspection period, which would give her time to have the building inspected and arrange for financing.

To avoid getting "scooped" by other interested buyers, Candace told her agent not to give the listing broker advance warning that their offer was coming in for fear that she would alert her prospective buyers. Another strategy they utilized was to have Candace's agent ask the listing broker if he could submit the offer directly to the RTC office in Chicago. No problem, the broker said. So the day after they walked through the property, he delivered the offer personally to the RTC office.

To everyone's immense surprise, (they had expected a counter offer of at least $600,000) the RTC quickly accepted the offer as it was. The deal was on.

Getting the Bucks

Next step: financing. Candace brought the president of a bank with which she had done business before over to see the property. He was so impressed that he approved a loan for $600,000—$50,000 more than the purchase price.

Candace found that working with the RTC on the purchase was not the frustrating experience she had feared it would be. For instance, between making the offer and signing the closing papers, something came up that had to be dealt with. The government had applied a deed restriction to the property for affordable housing. Thirty-five percent of the 19 units would have to be used for affordable housing. This restriction would run with the property for 40 years. However, if the property had not sold by January 25, that restriction would not apply. That is, anyone who tendered an offer after January 25 would not have to deal with the restriction. But the asking price would go up at that time because of the deletion of the restriction.

On its face, this wrinkle appeared to be a disaster. The property didn't fit the affordable housing profile. But Candace knew that if she waited until January 25 to resubmit her offer, she'd have to stand in line. Figuring that they'd have to live with the affordable housing deed restriction, Candace decided it was time to get all the information and explore options.

"I got in touch with my RTC contact in Chicago," she recalls, "and found that no one in the RTC office could tell me specifically what this restriction would mean. So we called for a meeting to iron things out, and we brought an attorney.

"The RTC people were very cooperative in setting up the meeting and trying to help us. They were not rude at all. They did not resist. They were willing to meet. They were willing to discuss. They were willing to solve the problem.

"When we sat down together, one of the RTC people there had just returned from a meeting at which the final affordable housing guidelines had been formulated. The impact on the property was that we would be required to set aside six of the existing 19 units as affordable housing apartments. We could decide which units. We would also be allowed to designate the units for senior citizens. They could all be in the old building, thereby allowing us to sell off the five existing townhouses. We would have to keep the main building as rentals, but we planned to do that anyway. Another important thing the RTC agreed to do was to give us two different deeds to the property—one for the property on which the existing buildings were located, and the other for the remaining property. This way, any future development we did would not fall under the deed restriction."

Acceptable Sacrifices

There happened to be six one-bedroom units in the main building. Assigning these smaller units affordable housing status would minimize the loss of rents, which would amount to about $55 per month for four units, and approximately $100 per month for the other two—acceptable sacrifices in light of the deal's overall potential.

Several investors in the area had been waiting for the deed restriction to run out on January 25 to make offers on the property. Once

Candace clarified the situation with the RTC, these investors were furious that the problem they had been waiting to avoid had turned out to be a paper tiger.

Some investors hadn't waited, however. Candace discovered that three other investors submitted offers to the RTC for the property as soon as they heard she had made an offer. At least one, she was told, was for considerably more than hers. "But the RTC took the offers in the order in which they were presented," she states.

"Also, they *liked us*. We were very careful and up-front with them in our dealings. We did what we said we would do. We provided them with proof that we could perform."

Getting on the RTC's good side continued to yield rewards for Candace and her partners. For instance, they readily agreed to extend the closing deadline by more than a month and a half past the 28-day inspection period because Candace was going to be in Europe.

The night before the closing, Candace's lawyer called her husband at his office and said that something was wrong because the numbers he was running for the closing showed that they should get a check at closing for $111,137. Howard assured him that nothing was wrong.

Candace and her contingency walked into the closing with their $600,000 bank loan and paid $525,000 cash (remember, they had already paid $25,000 as earnest money) for the property. This left them with $75,000. They also received their rent and tax prorations, tax credits, and the security deposits. After deducting the closing costs that accrued to them, they were given a check for *$111,137.93!*

Adding the Sizzle

From the $111,137 check, Candace reimbursed herself and her partners for the $12,500 they each put into the earnest money. They also paid themselves back for the out-of-pocket expenses they had incurred up to that date. The rest, they planned to use for repairs, decorating, landscaping, and engineering/architecture fees in connection with future development of the property.

In the seven weeks that they've owned the property, Candace and her partners have added many final touches—the sizzle that the limited partnership failed to add. Their efforts have paid off. Today, all 19 units are rented and the property is generating over $146,000 in annual gross rents—$24,000 more than when they purchased it.

Not only do they now own a property in which they have none of their own money (a property that would appraise today for over $2 million, and against which they only have a $600,000 mortgage); not only did they make more on the deal the very day they purchased it than many people make for a year's work, but they are also receiving a heady positive monthly cash flow.

How heady? Their monthly rental income is about $12,200. (Actually, it's more now, but would be that if all six of the designated affordable housing units were in fact rented at affordable housing levels.) Their monthly mortgage payment is less than $5,500. The monthly portion of property taxes (which they plan to have reduced based on their low purchase price) and insurance comes to less than $2,400. Add in some maintenance and repair costs, and there's still a healthy cash flow.

But that's only the beginning. "We're going to develop the property," explains Candace. "We'll be adding five townhouses in the front, which we'll start building next March. In all, we'll be building between 30 to 34 more townhouses on the property. It's already zoned for it, and over $100,000 was spent by a previous owner to bring the necessary improvements and utilities to the property.

Use Proper Channels

Candace has some suggestions for people who want to work effectively with the RTC. "I found that the people who alienated the RTC did not go through the proper channels," she explains. "They attempted to circumvent the RTC-appointed broker, were condescending toward RTC employees, and tried to bully senior RTC officials.

"You're not going to get anywhere—even if you're dead right—if you're not considerate and polite. I found that they would not be bullied. So play the game by their rules. Don't try to change them. Treat people with respect, and you'll be treated with respect. You'll get a lot more accomplished.

"I thought I had some good deals before this property, but this has definitely been my very best," she laughs. "In fact, we all look at it as the final cog in our retirement plans."

CHAPTER 30

The Good, the Bad, and the Ugly

Inner city Minneapolis is an area that many real estate investors won't touch. But Patty Johnson will. She has learned from first-hand experience that *good* profits can be made in *bad* neighborhoods from *ugly* houses.

From her residence in nearby Eden Prairie, Patty had been buying and selling residential real estate for years, when an investor friend tipped her off to a possible opportunity early in 1989.

It involved a house in inner city Minneapolis. He told Patty about it because he wanted nothing to do with it personally. The neighborhood was too bad, he said. In fact, he didn't even want to go there to check the property out.

"I jumped on it," recalls Patty, "and my husband and I went to take a look at it. It was a solid stucco house with natural woodwork. But it needed a lot of work. The lady selling it wanted $20,000 cash. She had lived there for a long time and wanted to get out of the area. She had gone through a divorce, and she was in poor health and couldn't do what needed to be done to keep it up.

"We went back and forth with her for several hours. I gave her the rundown on how much it was going to cost to fix up, and pointed out that homes weren't moving in the area as quickly as normal. I explained that I invested in real estate for a living and needed to make a profit."

Buying a Lower Purchase Price

Patty finally got her down to an $11,000 cash purchase price. She admits that she would never have been able to negotiate away almost half the original asking price if she hadn't taken the time to find out what the seller needed and wanted from the deal.

Primarily, the lady wanted cash to get into a new home. But she also wanted to be able to stay there and not move out until the first of August. This was May. Although delaying the closing for two and a half months made Patty nervous because it gave the seller plenty of time to change her mind, she agreed. Patty is convinced that this concession "bought" her the lower purchase price.

"In the art of negotiation," states Patty, "it's important to find out what the other parties' needs are. If you can figure out what they really want and what makes them tick, you've got a foot in the door."

The sales agreement was written up and signed in May. The long wait for the closing came to an end on August 1 without complications.

It took no great genius to realize that Patty had negotiated a good deal. The city had recently assessed the home, giving it a value of $55,000. (In the inner city of Minneapolis, the assessement is generally considered to be fairly close to the true market value.)

The Selling Point

Nevertheless, the home needed a lot of work. Recalls Patty: "It hadn't been painted in maybe 30 years. The lady, her husband, and their children had been smokers. The walls were literally orange-yellow. She had a lot of cats and there was a tremendous amount of animal odor. Beyond the obvious cosmetic improvements, the house needed roof repairs and electrical updating."

Patty, her husband, her teenage son, and his friend went to work. After cleaning, carpeting, painting, sanding the hardwood floors, and putting in new kitchen and bathroom floors, rewiring the electrical system, and repairing the roof, they had the home in good cosmetic shape.

It's important to find a focal point for the house that can be enhanced. "This house had a huge kitchen," she says. "It was ugly, but had real potential because of its size. We spent a lot of energy in the kitchen. We brightened it up, hung towels, and put a dish or two in the cupboards to make it look like home. It was the kitchen that eventually sold the house.

"Also, one of the selling points that I thought the house lacked was a garage," says Patty. "There had been a garage, but it burned down years ago. So I checked around for a used garage and found one that had to be moved because of a widening of a road or something like that. Buying and moving the garage cost only $700—a lot less than it would have taken to build one."

By the way, Patty uses a home equity line of credit when she needs to come up with cash to buy a house and fix it up. Because she usually has more than one of these flippers going at a time, cash is constantly flowing into and out of her bank accounts and line of credit loan.

All in all, the clean-up, repairs, and improvements cost Patty close to $14,000. Once they were completed, she listed the home with a real estate agent friend, then added the final touches.

All the Touches of Home

Final touches? After cleaning up and fixing up a *flipper* property like this, and before showing it, Patty dots the "i"'s and crosses the "t"'s by decorating it. She says: "Once we've done the carpeting, the painting, and all that, I go to garage sales. I get curtains, plant stands, pictures, and other decorations that I can buy for a buck or two at a garage sale. I also have silk plants that I cart from house to house when we put them on the market. It gives prospective buyers a homey feeling when they walk in."

Patty's system works, and worked quickly in this case. The first lady to walk through the house bought it. The sales price was *$56,000 cash.* That's $45,500 more than what she had paid for it.

After deducting $4,000 for the sales commission, $14,000 for repairs, interest expenses on the line of credit loan, closing costs, and all other expenses, Patty *netted $27,500* on this little house in two and a half months.

"I really think the key is decorating," she states. "It doesn't have to be a lot—just enough to help people focus on the decorating rather than any little flaw in the home. The addition of the garage was also a big factor in this case.''

The Extra Step

For Patty, this deal reconfirmed an important principle of real estate investing: Bad areas can be good opportunities, and ugly houses can create beautiful profits.

"There are usually a lot of government programs to help low-income people buy homes in these types of neighborhoods," she points out. "And if you get the neighbors on your side, you're not likely to have problems. The day we assumed the ownership of this house, we went knocking on the doors of the neighbors to find owner-occupants. We gave them all our phone numbers and asked them to please keep an eye out on the house because we had all our tools there.

"We didn't have one problem. Nothing was ever stolen. Nothing was ever damaged. In fact, it was extremely hot many of the days that we were working over there, and some of the neighbors would come over and bring pop. We felt safe there. I worked over there several days all by myself, and didn't feel uncomfortable at all.

"It just took that extra step to say 'Here we are. Here's what we're doing. We want to improve this house.' From that point on, it was easy."

CHAPTER 31

The Deal He Pulled Out of Thin Air

In Northern California there is a town named Redding. And in that town there is a real estate investor named Jay DeCima who has learned how to pull highly profitable real estate deals out of thin air . . . so to speak.

In 1980, Jay became interested in a run-down, 22-unit property in Redding. "It was a dirt-bag property," he says, "that was originally a motor lodge. These little units were situated on a very nice commercial property, 3½ acres in size. It was a hilly property with gently sloping contours and elevations that were very attractive. The cottages were about 300 square-feet each in size. They were little, self-contained living units—built in the early '40s—with either a kitchen, main room, and single bedroom, or a kitchen and a studio bedroom."

The property had fallen into a state of disrepair, and was the home of a few derelicts. Rental income, needless to say, was negligible. Every real estate person in Redding knew that this property was available, and most of them felt that it had potential. But no one seemed to know how to tap into that potential.

A Visual Concept

No one except Jay, that is. He visualized it as a senior citizens

137

development. Why not? The grass-covered park-like property offered plenty of room to get out and walk, and the units were small enough that they could be easily taken care of.

Jay saw a diamond in the rough. He knew that the small size of the individual cottages meant that they wouldn't require too much time or money to restore to good condition, and lent themselves to a one-by-one improvement plan.

"The problem was," laughs Jay, "I didn't have any money. I knew it wouldn't take much money to buy, but whatever it took was more than I had. I was already a real estate investor and landlord, but my financial resources were tied up in other properties."

Money was not the only problem, however. The city of Redding had already issued its first notice stating that it was going to close down and tear down the old motor lodge because it had spawned so many complaints about drug dealing and other undesirable activities. This added a sense of urgency to any plans investors might have had.

Making It Fly

Jay attacked the first problem—money—with the kind of financial creativity that has made him successful. "I happened to have a rental house," he explains, "that I had purchased a year earlier. I had paid $80,000 for the house with $20,000 down, and the seller carried a contract for the remaining $60,000. This house had potential for commercial development in the years ahead.

Negotiating with the seller of the 22-unit property, Jay discovered that he would accept equity in property in place of cash. So Jay decided to trade this particular rental home. "Magically," he says, "I made this house come to a value of $160,000 for the purposes of this trade. I basically pulled that figure out of thin air, thinking 'This will never fly!' But I made the offer and it *did* fly. The seller accepted my equity in that property, which, based on the $160,000 value and the $60,000 mortgage, was $100,000! The seller was obviously desperate."

Jay then assumed four existing mortgage notes on the property, which totaled about $140,000. The monthly mortgage payments on these notes was $1,280.

That was that. Jay had bought the property simply by assuming the four notes for $140,000 and giving the seller his rental home with its $60,000 mortgage—a house in which his actual dollar input had only been $20,000 for the purchase plus some fix-up costs.

The beauty of this deal can only be understood in light of the fact that the motor lodge property was listed for $240,000, which was a low, distressed price according to Jay's analysis.

But Jay's euphoria dissipated a bit when he discovered that the seller was behind in his mortgage payments, and that the property was in foreclosure. Plus, county taxes hadn't been paid for some time, and the local hardware store and lumber company had liens on the property for supplies he had purchased on credit.

"As this deal went along we had true confessions," remarks Jay. "At the beginning, I didn't know about all these problems. But as things progressed, the seller told me more and more. Of course, I found out about some of the problems when we did the preliminary title search.

"When we figured out where we actually stood on this property, I realized that this guy was in a heap of financial trouble. I also realized that I would have at least $100,000 equity in the property the moment I bought it. So I arranged to go get a loan against that $100,000 equity—I had good credit—and *give the seller a loan of $25,000 to pay everything off and unencumber the property.* I would then put a five-year, interest-only trust deed for that $25,000 back on the rental house that I was giving him in the trade."

New Meaning

This gave new meaning to the term *seller financing.*

As it turned out, Jay borrowed not just $25,000, but $50,000 from a finance company. He made the $25,000 loan to the seller and held the other $25,000 away to fix up the 22 units.

By the time Jay closed on the purchase of the old motor lodge, all the delinquent mortgage payments, liens, and back taxes had been paid off and cleared up. At that point in time, he owned a property worth at least $240,000, with about $140,000 in notes against it, plus the $50,000 he had just borrowed. He also owned a $25,000 note secured by the rental house he had traded to buy the property. And he had $25,000 to renovate the 22 units.

What had all this actually cost him? Just his equity in the rental house which he had traded—an equity that had cost him just a little more than $20,000 to achieve.

In short, for just over $20,000, Jay had "purchased" a $50,000 equity in the 22-unit property (its $240,000 value minus the $140,000 and the $50,000 in loans), plus a $25,000 interest-bearing mortgage note, plus $25,000 in cash (his fix-up fund).

"What made this work," Jay quickly points out, "is that this guy was in a corner with no place to go, and it was obvious that he could not handle this kind of property."

Keeping the City at Bay

That's how Jay overcame the "no money" problem. But what about problem number two? Remember, the city had already issued a notice that it was going to tear down the 22 units. Jay admits that this is the problem which had scared other investors away. Everyone was afraid that the city would tear the cottages down before they could do anything about it.

Jay was more confident. He already had experience working with city and HUD officials, and knew that housing was in short supply in Redding. Still, it wasn't smooth sailing. His first meeting with the city committee that was handling the condemnation of the property was tense. The committee basically said, "We've been through this with previous owners of the motor lodge, and we're not going to mess with you, Jay. If you don't have it done in 60 days, it goes."

Jay took an attorney with him to the next meeting. The lawyer's arguments and subtle references to possible lawsuits bought him time: six months (which was later extended to a year).

Jay, and a handyman he had hired, physically moved onto the property and went to work. It was a mess. The pool was filled with beer cans. Weeds grew like trees. The cottages were eyesores. But their clean up efforts soon began to make a difference. The work went on for a year. In addition to cleaning up, fixing up, and renovating, a few big ticket items had to be dealt with, such as installing an underground power delivery system and hooking up to the city water system (the units had been served by an on-site well).

All in all, it took close to $50,000 and one year's time to whip the property into shape. The money Jay spent beyond the $25,000 restoration fund he had set aside came from his pocket and cash flow, stretching his credit thin.

No Eviction Necessary

From the very beginning, there was enough rental income to cover the monthly mortgage payments. But these rents came largely from unmanageable tenants. Says Jay: "The question was not 'Will we have enough rent to sustain this project?'; but 'Will we live through the night?' A lot went on. The police were coming out two or three times a night for disturbances, chasing drunks to their cottages, and so on.

"But I learned a good lesson here. I learned that the kind of tenants you don't want will leave when the sun hits them. The shady tenants want to live in something that doesn't look lived in. They want to be hidden. When you begin to work with rakes and tools at 8:00 a.m., you disrupt their life-style. They move. When you cut down the weeds enough to let the sunlight hit them, they move. You don't have to evict them."

Not surprisingly, many of the renters that were living there drifted off soon after Jay and his handyman moved in. As they fixed up the cottages, they attracted more manageable tenants, and Jay positioned the property as a conveniently located senior citizen's rental community—a place where seniors got a discount and could even have a pet (the only place in town that allowed this).

"In 1981 the city came out and took pictures," recalls Jay. "There was an article in the paper saying how proud the city was that there was now a wonderful place for seniors, and bragging about how they had cooperated with me. There were a lot of favorable comments from other sources, too, about Hillside Cottages. (That's what I named it.) In fact, whenever I have to prove my credibility I can point to Hillside and that's all it takes."

About two years after buying Hillside Cottages, Jay decided to sell it. By that time it was a nice, modest, rental community for seniors that was generating $3,800 to $4,000 gross rental income per month.

Without listing the property, Jay sold Hillside Cottages for

$425,000 in 1982. There was a $50,000 cash down payment, and the four notes that Jay had assumed from the previous owner (which now totaled about $130,000) were wrapped with a mortgage note which Jay carried for the remaining $375,000 of the sales price. The interest was 12 percent.

A Fine Nest Egg

Although Jay's many real estate investments kept his finances in a state of flux, with funds constantly being moved in and out of projects, on a theoretical level it could be said that the $50,000 down payment from selling Hillside repaid the $50,000 loan he received from the finance compny. That left him with a 12 percent mortgage note for $375,000, from which he had to pay the four notes worth about $130,000. Subtracting the $130,000 from the $375,000, we find that Jay "owned" $245,000 of the wrapped note. Plus, he was making money on the interest spread between 12 percent and the lower rates of the wrapped notes.

In addition, he still had the $25,000 note for the loan he had made to the man who sold him the motor lodge in the first place—a note that was earning interest and would come due in '85. Some of that $25,000, however, would theoretically be offset by the extra money he had put into the renovation above and beyond cash flow.

"What's nice is that I virtually pulled this deal out of thin air," says Jay.

In the final analysis, using creativity and sweat equity, Jay turned his Hillside Cottages investment (which originally cost him just over $20,000 equity in a traded rental house) into a nest egg worth somewhere in the neighborhood of a quarter million dollars.

That's a great neighborhood to be in.

CHAPTER 32

The In-Flight Deal
That Almost Crashed

"The story of my best deal starts back in my ego days," says Mark Haroldsen.

It was 1979. I had chartered a Lear Jet to fly from Chicago to Lansing, Michigan, where I was giving a speech. The press was going to be there at the airport waiting for me, so I thought, "Hey, I'm going to dazzle these guys and fly in on a jet!"

We arrived early, so we had to circle for half an hour waiting for the press to arrive before we could land. I wanted to get my money's worth out of the jet. While we were still in the air I heard a phone ring and the pilot said, "It's for you, Mr. Haroldsen."

I thought, "Who would be calling me up here?" It happened to be David Cowan, whom I had hired to manage my real estate and find new properties. He told me he had found a property in Charlotte, North Carolina, that consisted of 102 townhouses. He went over the numbers and the deal sounded good. (As it turned out, it sounded much better than it turned out to be. But that's not unusual.)

There I was in this Lear Jet with a big ego and an entourage of people who were listening to my side of the converesation. So I had to put on my Master of the Universe voice and say, "Sure. Buy that property! Put $100,000 down. Pay up to $1 millon.Yeah,do that deal, Baby!"

Dave went ahead and bought the townhouse property, called Westchester Townhouses, per my instructions. The purchase price was $985,000. (They had been asking about $1.3 million.) I made $100,000 cash down payment, which came from my own funds. For the $885,000 balance, I assumed two existing mortgages.

Things I Hadn't Expected

It was one thing to sit there in a corporate jet trying to impress a lot of people and say "Buy!" But it was an entirely different thing to stand there with my feet in the dirt looking at a rundown, mismanaged property for which I had just paid close to a million dollars.

As it turned out, we had to put another $60,000 into fixing it up. This was something I hadn't expected. To make matters worse, the market was very soft there during that period, and we were running a 20-plus percent vacancy rate. I got a call one night saying someone had been shotgunned to death in his apartment. That sort of thing will empty a building out real fast.

All in all, we were running a big negative cash flow—which was something else I hadn't expected. The worst problem we had there was poor management. We went through several managers. It was painful. One manager said he was doing a good job and everything was under control. Being 2,000 miles away, we took his word for it . . . for a while at least. I finally had someone go check this guy out. It turned out that he wasn't even there during the day. He was going to school.

The property took a huge bite out of me, both financially and psychologically. I mean, when you're thinking you're the smartest man in the universe and then you do something stupid, you suddenly have to step back and say, "Wait a minute! I'm mortal! Maybe I'm not so smart after all."

The Beginning of Change

I thought I had made a *big* mistake. I was mad at everyone. I was mad at Dave for finding the deal. I was mad at myself for letting my ego get me into it that day in the jet.

But I hung on and eventually things began to change. We were finally able to find a good manager, stabilize things, and get the vacancy rate down to almost zero. We also got the place looking quite nice. Our fix-up work started on the outside and worked its way in. This enabled us to gradually raise rents.

It took two years to turn the property around to where things were running smoothly and we were seeing a positive cash flow. I'll admit, during most of that period I never thought I'd see the day when the property would stop being a problem and start being a money-maker. But we made it happen.

After another four years I decided to sell Westchester. By then—by mid-1986—it was a very different property than the one we had purchased. We had taken a problem property and had created an attractive, well-run piece of real estate with a good track record and a healthy positive cash flow. We sent out letters to approximately 900 syndicators throughout the United States, and sold it to one of them on August 1 for *over $2.5 million!*

The syndicate paid me $500,000 down and assumed the two existing mortgages I had assumed six years earlier. I then carried back a 10-year, interest-only mortgage note for the balance of $1,185,640. This 9½ percent note was payable at *$9,386 per month.* I'm still receiving that $9,386 each month, and will for another four years until the time the $1,185,640 balance comes due.

When the syndicate gave me the $500,000 cash down payment, the positive cash flow I had been getting for roughly four years had paid me back a sizeable chunk of the money I had invested in the property, which included the $100,000 down payment, the $60,000 improvement costs, and the earlier negative cash flow I had to cover. But it hadn't paid back all of those costs.

Still, the $500,000 payment immediately gave me an approximate $380,000 profit on the deal. In addition, I owned the $1,185,640 mortgage note on the property. I would get the full $1,185,640 in ten years. And while I waited, I would receive $9,386 interest payments on the note each and every month for ten years! *Those interest payments alone would total $1,126,320!*

High-Flying Ego

Although this venture isn't the most profitable real estate deal I've ever done in terms of sheer dollars and cents, I've always thought of it as my *best* deal because of the story surrounding it—my high-flying ego and so on—and because of the lessons it taught me.

For instance, it taught me never to make deals on Lear jets; but if you do, hang in there until you can turn things around. It also taught me that a single real estate transaction can produce a string of unforeseen benefits. When we make a real estate investment, we often don't realize what will come out of the funnel at a later date. At the onset we see only the tip of the iceberg.

An Update

This is exactly what happened with this deal. In March, 1991, the buyer came back to me and wanted to renegotiate the payments on the $1,185,640 note. He wanted to reduce the payments and let interest accrue because they were having some problems, and pay me an incentive to do so. I said I wouldn't do that, but that I would loan him the money to pay off the existing first mortgage his syndicate has assumed, which had been paid down to quite a low balance, though the monthly payments were still high. (They had paid off the second assumed mortgage by that time.) So they were able to reduce their monthly payments, and I was able to make a mortgage loan at a very attractive interest rate. This meant that I held both the first and the second mortgages on the property.

In short, the deals that spin off from an initial transaction can be very profitable—in some cases, more profitable than the original deal. Someone looking at what happened with the Westchester property might say, "This guy's a genius! How did he figure all this out?" The fact is, I'm not a genius. I could never have initially figured out all the nuances and side deals that came with the unfolding of time and events.

That's just one of the many beauties of real estate.

CHAPTER 33

Pushing a Deal to Its Limits

You never know how good a deal can get until you push it to its limits. Philadelphia investor Craig Emrey discovered this early in his income property career.

In 1988 Craig put an ad in the newspaper that read, "We buy homes. Tell us what you want." Someone called who had inherited a single-family, attached row home in South Philadelphia from his family. There was a $20,000 mortgage on the home. The seller wanted to get $10,000 cash out of the property so he could move to California.

"I looked at the property," recalls Craig. "It was in immaculate condition. Two guys were renting the home for $600 a month. So I decided to go ahead with the deal and structure the sale around the seller's needs."

Working with the owner, Craig negotiated a $40,000 sales price. This, however, was contingent on the home appraising for $52,900, which included an extra $2,000 to $3,000 for its excellent condition.

Stamp of Approval

The seller said he wanted to have his attorney look at the agreement before signing it. This worried Craig—not because there was anything wrong with the deal in any way—but because he knew that lawyers are often skeptical about no-down, over-financed sales . . .

147

which this was. When the attorney gave the deal his stamp of approval, Craig was relieved and more than a little surprised.

"Back then," explains Craig, "they had 80 percent investor *no-doc* loans. They really only looked at your credit report. You didn't even need to show them your past few years' tax returns. And they would lend you up to 80 percent of the appraised value of the property."

Craig was right on the money. The home appraised for—surprise?—$52,900, and Craig got a 30-year loan for 80 percent of that amount, or $42,320.

With that money, Craig purchased the South Philly home for himself and a partner for the agreed-upon $40,000. Why did the seller agree to a price that was $12,900 under the appraised value? The answer is simple: Craig figured out what he wanted and made sure he got it.

Lining Up the Numbers

Here's how the numbers lined up at the closing: From the $42,320 loan proceeds, the $20,000 existing mortgage was paid off; $10,000 cash went to the seller; and closing costs (which are high in Philadelphia, according to Craig) were paid to the tune of $5,180.

That left $7,140 on the table and a balance of $10,000 to pay to the seller (the $40,000 sales price, minus the $10,000 cash payment, minus the $20,000 that paid off the existing mortgage).

"This is the kicker," states Craig. "The seller took back a five-year, 10 percent interest, *no payment* note for the $10,000 balance. You see, he really only wanted the $10,000. So I structured it in a way that he would get that, but I would get what I wanted, too—namely, to walk away from the closing with more money in my pocket than I walked in with, rather than vice versa. So *instead of having to pay $2,860 at the closing, I walked away with $7,140 in cash.*"

Better still, the property Craig was "paid" $7,140 to buy was producing a nice positive cash flow. The tenants (who are still there) are model renters who pay utilities and up to $50 per month in repair costs in addition to rent. Craig pays taxes and insurance on the home, which, together with the principle and interest payments on the $42,320 loan add up to a monthly expense of $475. With a rent of

$610, Craig and his partner realize $135 of positive cash flow each month.

"Basically, I was trying to see how far I could push this deal," says Craig. "I was having fun with it, and it worked."

What about the $10,000 second mortgage note that will have to be paid to the seller in '93? Craig already has this angle worked out. The two tenants who have rented the house since before Craig and his partner purchased it want to buy it. This suits Craig's plans perfectly.

"I don't want to have to come up with the $10,000 plus accrued interest when the note comes due," Craig explains. "So my game plan is to sell it to the tenants just before the due date. My conservative estimate of what the home will be worth then is $60,000, more or less."

Granted, after paying off the $10,000 second mortgage loan with accrued interest, plus the first mortgage (which will have been paid down only slightly after five years), Craig won't clear enough on the sale to make him or his partner rich—probably just a few thousand dollars after closing costs have been paid.

The Value of Terms

But the true value of this deal must be assessed in terms of what Craig put into it as opposed to what he has and will take out of it.

What he put into it was this: a very small amount of his time and *no* money. What he (and his partner) took out of it was this: $7,140 cash the day he bought it. Plus, by the time they sell the home, they will have taken an average of $135 per month positive cash flow out of it for five years. That's $8,100.

Already, that's a $15,240 profit on zero dollars invested. (Technically, this represents an infinite rate of return.) So even if Craig only clears a few thousand dollars when he sells the home, he and his partner won't go to the bank crying.

"When I think of the time-value of money," he says, "I realize how beneficial it was to have taken a big chunk of the profits out of this deal up front, rather than wait five years.

"I've done many, many deals," Craig concludes. "But this was a truly classic no-money-down deal where the buyer walks away from the closing with cash in his pocket and a property that generates a positive cash flow. And all it took was a little creative pushing."

CHAPTER 34

Profits in the Midst of Chaos

Some deals are sweet and simple. Some are sweet and chaotic. Florida investor Brad Banta's best deal definitely falls into the latter category.

It involves a 106-unit apartment complex in Brad's city of residence: Ft. Lauderdale. The property consists of six 2-story buildings which break down into four 1-bedroom units, sixteen 3-bedrom units, and 86 two-bedroom units.

Schooled to Deal

Originally built as an apartment building, the property was purchased in 1982 by Bauder College, a community college located adjacent to it. It had been used since then as a student dormitory. The college and the property were owned by National Education Centers (NEC), one of the largest private school owners in the nation—if not the largest.

"The college administrators decided that they didn't like managing real estate," says Brad. "They wanted to run their school. A broker who had brought me three other properties told me about it. I liked the looks of it, so I made my first offer in July, 1988.

"They were asking $3.2 million, and I offered $2.6 million, or about $2.9 million if they would accept a small down payment and finance the balance. The college owned the apartments free and clear, by the way.

"I thought I had a deal clinched, but the person I was dealing with left the college. He didn't tell anyone about his dealings with me, so my broker and I had to start all over again with a new person. We ended up working with three different people before finding one that stuck to it and got the deal done."

Luckily, Brad's broker was tenacious, because it took almost two years—until May, 1990—to get a sales agreement signed.

The property was in slightly below-average condition when Brad first negotiated for it in '88. It needed landscape work and paint. In the following two years the college did nothing, so by the time Brad's offer was accepted, it needed a substantial amount of work.

"We agreed on a price of $3.55 million, with a $350,000 credit for needed repairs," recalls Brad. "This was more of a maneuver to make the property look better to lenders than anything else. So really, the net sales price was $3.2 million. I would get a new first mortgage loan of $2.56 million, which I would give them as a cash payment. They would hold the rest of the balance of $640,000 in a five-year second mortgage note at 10 percent interest, with interest-only payments.

Falling Apart at the Financing

The closing was set for July, 1990. That gave Brad two months to find $2.56 million. He found a mortgage banker who said he could find the money for him, but would need $15,000 initially to get the ball rolling. Brad and the college each agreed to pay half this amount. They would also need a survey and appraisal. The college agreed to pay for these.

July came and went, and the mortgage banker hadn't come up with the money, notwithstanding his assurances that it would be available "any day." August came and went, as did September. Says Brad: "He kept giving us the runaround. Instead of acting as a mortgage *banker*, he was really just a mortgage *broker*, and his source dried up. He just didn't want to tell us. In October, we figured it out and the deal fell apart from lack of financing."

Brad hadn't put all his eggs in one basket, though. He had gone to another mortgage banker. This one said he would make the $2.56 million loan, but would hold back $1 million of it until the necessary repairs were made.

The college agreed to this and the deal was on again . . . until the president of the company got fired. Once again, the one-again-off-again deal was off.

"It finally hit us," explains Brad, "that the problem with this deal was the property. The condition was such that everyone we went to for money said, 'Sure, we'll lend you the money. Fix the property up, then you'll get your money.'

"So we decided to go back through the property—right down to inspecting each individual unit—and we made a three-page list of everything we saw wrong with it, including how many refrigerators and air-conditioners needed to be replaced, what had to be done with the roof and the landscaping, and so on. We showed the list to our contact at the college and showed him that there was currently $435,000 worth of repairs to be done in addition to the original estimate of $350,000. We told him that we were willing to proceed, but that we wanted that much more of a credit for repairs. The contact said he'd look at it and get back to us.

Looking at Both Sides

"The next day he called us and said, 'This is what we'll do. We'll give you a second credit for $265,000—not the $435,000 you've asked for. This will be in addition to the first credit for $350,000 that we already agreed on.'

"This guy was a straight-shooter. He would look at the situation from both of our perspectives and decide what was fair. From that point forward, there wasn't much room for negotiation. In this case that was fine, because I would have accepted much less than the extra $265,000 credit."

Toward the end of '90 the deal was back on and an agreement was signed. The sales price was still $3.55 million with the $350,000 repair credit, making the net price $3.2 million. In another paragraph, the college gave Brad the additional $265,000 in repair credit—but did it in an interesting way.

"The deal we worked out is that I would get a $265,000 first mortgage from a bank to cover that second repair credit. But the money wouldn't go to the seller. It would go to *me* for the fix-up. The college would then carry back the entire balance of the purchase price ($2,935,000) in two different notes."

The first note would be a five-year, interest-only, $640,000 second mortgage at 10 percent interest. This was the same arrangement that had been made on the earlier agreement.

But now, the college was willing to go further to make the transaction work. It would carry a temporary, interest only, purchase-money mortgage note for the remaining $2,295,000 for a few years until Brad could obtain outside financing. The interest on this note would be 8.5 percent the first year, prime rate the second year, and prime plus 2 percent the third year. It was the intention of both parties that this note would be refinanced and paid off by the end of the second year, but the third year was thrown in as a buffer in case Brad needed more time to get the loan.

Something happened before closing to slightly alter these numbers. Certain repairs had to be made before the new school quarter began—$38,000 worth. This would have to be done before the closing. Since the college wasn't set up to do this work and Brad was, he got his crew to do the repairs and the college paid him $38,000 for it. This arrangement assured Brad that the work would be done to his satisfaction.

Juggling the Numbers

Because this work would have been paid for out of his $265,000 repairs credit, which was to be in the form of a first mortgage that Brad was going to keep to do the work, and because the college paid for it before the closing, the $265,000 credit was reduced by $38,000 to $227,000. To keep things fair, the $38,000 was then added to the $2,295,000 note which the college was going to carry back temporarily, making that note $2,333,000.

When getting the long-term financing to pay off this $2,333,000 note, Brad would also need to pay off the $227,000 variable-rate first mortgage from the bank. So he would need to borrow $2,560,000. "That shouldn't be hard to do once we get the property fixed up and get the rental income where it should be," he asserts.

Another aspect of the deal relates to the $640,000 five-year, interest-only note the college agreed to hold. It was agreed that when Brad gets the loan to pay off the other $2,333,000 seller-held note and the $227,000 bank mortgage, the $640,000 note will become subordinated to the new $2,560,000 note. But if Brad can borrow enough to pay off the $640,000 note too, the college will give him a 2 percent per year discount for early payment.

The college also agreed to pay the closing expenses.

It was a two-day closing—February 21 and 22, 1991. The college representatives had to bring $265,132 to the closing. They paid $9,513 for the documentary stamps on the notes, which is usually paid by the buyer, as well as $5,946 intangible tax on the mortgage and $13,325 for Brad's title insurance. Prior to the closing, they had paid $1,250 for the survey and $2,500 for the appraisal.

"The one nobody can believe," says Brad, "is that they paid $20,000 of *my* attorney's $24,110 fee, which was a reasonable bill given the fact that the deal was so complex and lengthy."

The remainder of the $265,132 paid the other normal (and in this case, substantial) expenses that accrued to the seller, including their own attorney's fees and prorations (rent, security deposits, taxes, etc.).

Yet Another Twist

The payment of the real estate broker's commission adds yet another twist to this intricate transaction. The college representative had earlier negotiated the commission down to $125,000. He had also proposed that the commission be paid out of the interest payments Brad would be making to the college, but the broker would not accept this.

To prevent an impasse, Brad said that he would pay the $125,000 broker's commission the closing on behalf of the college, and then pay himself back by keeping the interest payments he would otherwise be making to the college for eight months. This was agreeable to both parties.

When the dust settled after the two-day closing, Brad walked away with $14,998 cash and $227,000 in an escrow account to be used to fix up the property, for which he would have to make monthly payments of approximately $2,000. ("The $227,000 should be fairly close to all we need," says Brad.) Of course, he also owned the property, encumbered by the $227,000 bank mortgage and the college's two mortgage notes already described.

The college walked away from the closing $265,132 and one property poorer, but with two valuable mortgage notes in hand worth close to $3 million.

It should be pointed out that the $14,998 cash which Brad received at the closing was a net amount, after he had paid or repaid *all* his own expenses in the deal to date, including the remaining $4,110 he owed to his attorney, his half of the fee to the mortgage broker ($7,500), and the costs of inspecting the property.

"The reason we walked away with *only* $14,998 at the closing," explains Brad, "is that we fronted the $125,000 commission for the seller. Otherwise, we would have taken $139,998 away from the table. But because of that we didn't have to make interest payments to the college for eight months.

"So what started out being a cash deal to the seller ended up being a cash deal to *me.*"

Owning a Piece of the Pie

Immediately upon taking over the property, Brad unleashed his management machine on the 106-unit apartment complex. He brought in an on-site manager couple that had been with him for years, as well as a trusted maintenance supervisor, and gave both the couple and the supervisor 10 percent ownership shares of the property.

"They put up their 10 percent share of what it took to get into the property," Brad quips. "Ten percent of nothing is nothing." Obviously, Brad believes people do their best work when they own a piece of the pie.

This is proving to be true in this case. The property and its management have already been greatly improved. Less than a half-year after the closing, most of the physical repairs and upgrades have been made, with the rest scheduled for completion within the coming two months. Rent increases of $15 per quarter per student are planned. To raise the occupancy rate, plans are being made to rent units not used by students to non-student tenants.

In July, 1990—over a half year before the closing—the property appraised for $3.6 million. With over a quarter-million dollars of improvements and an efficient property management machine in place, it can be conservatively assumed that the real estate will have appreciated to the $4 million mark, or higher, within a year's time—over *a million dollars more* than the $2,935,000 net price for which Brad purchased it ($3,550,000 minus credits for repairs of $350,000 and $265,000.)

Worth a Pretty Penny

What about cash flow? When Brad assumed ownership there were 230 student tenants, each paying $620 per quarter. This is an average number of renters per quarter. There are four quarters in the school year. That's an average gross rental income of $570,400 per year, or $47,533 per month.

Let's say in a few months Brad were to get a new loan of $3.2 millon to completely pay off the three existing mortgage notes on the property ($2,333,000, $640,000, and $227,000). Let's also say that this new loan will be a 20-year term, 11 percent interest loan. The monthly payments on this loan would be $33,030. Even if Brad didn't improve the occupancy rate or raise rents, the $47,533-per-month gross rental income would give him $14,503 per month over and above debt service costs to pay all other utility and management costs.

Clearly, his net positive cash flow would be lucrative even on that basis. When increased occupancy and rent levels are thrown into the equation, it becomes equally clear that Brad has created a gold mine out of a troubled piece of real estate and a marathon deal that took almost three years to bring to reality.

His plans? "We'll probably hang onto it for four or five years," Brad conjectures. "By then it will be worth a pretty penny."

CHAPTER 35

"It Ain't Over 'til It's Over"

The popular sporting phrase, "It ain't over 'til it's over," applies to real estate deals as well as it does to baseball games. Mark Ward, jet-fighter-pilot-turned-real-estate-investor can prove it.

The proof is his best deal—a series of transactions that threatened in the early innings to lead to a serious defeat, but turned into a big win by the end of the game.

Mark, a graduate of the Air Force Academy, began buying investment real estate while still on active duty. Toward the end of 1985 a classified newspaper ad drew his attention to a property consisting of four older houses on a fairly rural five-acre parcel of land in Apple Valley, California—a neighboring community to Victorville, his town of residence.

A Fixer in the Making

One house was a three-bedroom home with its own water-well and electric meter. The other three—two 2-bedroom homes and one 1-bedroom home—were hooked up to the same well and the same electric meter. All four houses had tenants, but both the tenants and the property needed fixing up. "It was overgrown, there were junk cars, and the homes themselves were a mess,'' says Mark.

The seller was asking $125,000, with $20,000 down. Working through his real estate agent, Mark offered $110,000 with $10,000 down. The offer was rejected.

"I went back out to the property," recalls Mark, "and there was something that told me that it was a diamond in the rough. So I decided to offer exactly what the seller was asking: $125,000 with $20,000 cash down, and the seller would carry an all-inclusive trust deed (wraparound) for the $105,000 balance. There happened to be an existing first mortgage of about $55,000 on the property (10 percent interest), and he could wrap it at 10½ percent interest. I would make monthly payments of $1,050 until the $105,000 was paid in about 20 years."

After making this offer, Mark had to go to Cairo to fly an Egyptian F-4 Phantom jet to the United States. While he was gone, his full-price, full-terms offer was rejected. Faced with the full offer, the seller suddenly thought he'd priced the property too low. The brokers, agents, and Mark threatened legal action, and finally, in January of '86, the seller complied and the deal was consummated. Mark raised the $20,000 cash down payment by borrowing against several of his credit cards.

A Real Rat's Nest

The rents were low—even for the houses' rundown conditions. The three-bedroom home was renting for $350 per month; the two-bedrooms for $200 and $195; and the one-bedroom for $175. Mark discovered that the seller had an arrangement with the tenants. He would not raise their rents if they did all their own repairs and never called him. They kept their part of the bargain: they never called him. But they didn't do any of the needed repairs. Hence, the property had become a rat's nest.

"Shortly after the closing," recalls Mark, "two nightmarish things happened. The first thing was that I got calls from three of the tenants within about a ten-minute time frame saying that the electricity had been turned off. The previous owner hadn't told me that both two-bedroom homes plus the one-bedroom house were all on the same electric meter . . . and he was paying the monthly bill. So he took it out of his name and they shut it down. I immediately had it put in my name. The trouble was, when I got the first bill, it was for about $500. This was in the winter, and because the tenants weren't paying for electricity, they had disconnected the propane heating system and were using space heaters in all the rooms. Their places were like the tropics.

"The second shock I got was when I went to collect the rents the first time. The tenants, who were all good friends, had gotten together and decided that they were not going to pay me. They were quite jovial about it, really. They just said that they were all buddies, and Joe across the street said he wasn't going to pay, so why should they; and Xavier over there said he wasn't going to pay because things needed to be fixed and his electricity got shut off, and when they went over, his beer was warm, so none of them felt like they should pay the rent."

Mark went home and prepared four 3-day notices to pay rent or quit. He also prepared a 30-day notice to increase the rents. He had planned to do that anyway, and figured that if they were going to have a battle, they might as well get it all over with right then. The three-bedroom home would rent for $450, the two 2-bedroom homes for $325, and the one-bedroom house for $275. This would increase his gross rental income from $920 to $1,375 per month.

"I went back out the same day,' says Mark, who mentions that beer cans and motorcycles were the property's most prominent landscaping motifs at the time. "When they saw me they all gathered around. I handed each of them their two notices and said, 'Read these over. You have three days to pay your rent. You will deliver it to me in person. If you don't, I'll be filing in court. I really don't care if you stay or go. I can get a lot more rent than even this. If you pay, I'll think about starting to fix some things maybe in a month or so when I get some time.'

"Their jaws dropped to the ground, and I walked away. The next day, one of the tenants brought me all their rents."

Why God Made Credit Cards

It was three weeks later that Mark got the $500 electric bill for the three houses that were on the same meter. (The other house was on a separate meter and that tenant paid his own electric bill.)

Realizing that something had to be done—not only to the electric meter situation but also to the overall image of the property—mark got out his credit cards, borrowed $15,000, got a crew together, and went to work.

After one month and $15,000, Mark had the four houses in top shape. The repairs had been made. The homes looked great. Each was on its own electric meter.

At this point, Mark told the tenants that they would be paying for their own electric costs. He also gave them 30-day notices of rent increases based on the improved condition of the property. The three-bedroom home would rent for $600, the two 2-bedroom homes for $475, and the one-bedroom house for $385. This meant that the new gross rental income would shoot from $1,375 to $1,935 per month.

Says Mark: "Now I'm thinking, 'These guys are either going to move, or they're going to refuse to pay me.' They refused to pay me. They called me to come out and meet with them. They were all there sitting around drinking beer. 'We're not going to pay you because now you're getting greedy,' they said. I pointed out that the new rents weren't at all out of line, and gave them another three-day notice to quit or pay rent. Three days later the same representative brought me all the rent. It was a poker game."

With the higher rents, Mark cut his negative cash flow down to almost nothing. (He was paying the $1,050 monthly mortgage payment, close to $600 per month on the $35,000 he had borrowed from his credit card accounts, plus taxes, insurance, and a few miscellaneous costs, such as the electricity for one of the two wells.) Still, the property was not making money.

Making His Moves

It was time to make his move—a move he had anticipated since he first saw the property. Mark set the wheels in motion to make a four-way lot split. The property qualified as a *minor subdivision,* which involves much less work than a regular subdivision.

He subdivided the five-acre property into four 1¼-acre parcels. On one were the three smaller homes with their well. On another was the three-bedroom home and its well. This left two vacant 1¼-acre parcels. The total cost of the subdivision at that time was roughly $2,000. It would prove to be the best $2,000 Mark had ever spent.

Subdividing the land was only the first step of Mark's plan. The second step was critical: he had to persuade the first and second mortgage holders to take their mortgages off the entire property and apply them to just one of the lots. This way, Mark would own the remaining lots free and clear.

It took some doing, but Mark pulled it off. Based on the increased value of the property, he persuaded the man who held the $55,000 first mortgage note (which had been wrapped by the $105,000 note) to move that note to the three-bedroom house and its 1¼-acre parcel. Simultaneously, Mark persuaded the holder of the $105,000 second mortgage wraparound note to take the $50,000 equity he had in the note ($105,000 minus the $55,000 that it wrapped), split it into two $25,000 notes, and move those onto the two vacant 1¼-parcels. Mark had to give him an extra quarter percent interest to do this.

When these negotiations were finished, the lot with the three-bedroom house had a $55,000 mortgage against it. Each of the two vacant lots had a $25,000 mortgage against it. The lot with the three houses was free and clear.

In addition, Mark had a $35,000 bill on his credit cards to clear up, which he had incurred for the down payment and improvements. Plus, he had to reimburse himself for some out-of-pocket expenses with which he had covered the negative cash flow during the first few months of ownership.

Paying Myself Back

While Mark was getting the mortgages moved around, he found a buyer for the three houses on the one 1¼-acre lot. The buyer agreed to pay $125,000 cash, within $5,000 of what Mark was asking.

"With the $125,000 cash," reminisces Mark, "I paid off my credit cards for the $20,000 down payment and the $15,000 fix-up costs, and I reimbursed myself for my other expenses, including some negative cash flow and the subdivision fees. *After paying myself back every dollar I had put into the deal, I had roughly $85,000 in cash profits left over, plus the three remaining properties."*

Mark used the $85,000 cash well. He made a down payment on a

$750,000 25-unit apartment building, and went to the Greek Islands.

He also put the three-bedroom house and the two vacant lots he still owned to good use. He was paying about $225 per month on each of the two vacant lot mortgages, and close to $450 per month on the house mortgage. "I was making a slight positive cash flow on the home, since it was renting for $600 per month," states Mark, "but I didn't want to have to pay $550 a month for two pieces of dirt. I hate negative cash flows.

"So I started looking around town, and found a boarded-up, four-unit property (a 2-bedroom house, a duplex, and a single-unit in the back) in Victorville. I learned that these were owned by a sophisticated investor in Laguna Beach, and that this same man owned another 2-unit property just a few blocks away which was also in trouble and on the verge of condemnation. All six units—both properties—were under some sort of a blanket mortgage."

Let's Do an Exchange

Smelling a motivated seller, Mark contacted the Laguna Beach owner and suggested a 1031 tax-deferred exchange. He would trade his virtually self-running three-bedroom house and two 1½-acre lots in Apple Valley for the gentleman's six units in Victorville.

The owner of the Victorville properties agreed. But because his six units were worth more than Mark's house and lots, he would take back a note for the difference, or "boot." In deciding what the boot would be, the two parties disagreed on the value of Mark's properties. Mark said he felt that the house was worth $90,000 and each lot was worth $40,000. The investor said he thought Mark was crazy.

"Okay," said Mark, "if you want to get an appraisal, that's fine with me, but here's the game: If we get an appraisal, we go with whatever the appraisal says." The investor agreed.

To Mark's delight, the appraisal came in at $100,000 for the house, and $45,000 each for the lots. The investor tried to renege, but Mark held firm. "I'm sorry, but this was the deal," he said. You decided to get a little greedy and it bit you. Either we're going to do this as agreed, or we won't do it at all."

The deal went through . . . as agreed. Mark would get the six Victorville units which were free and clear except for a $22,000, 8 percent mortgage note on the 2-unit property (monthly payments of $225). The Laguna Beach investor would take Mark's three properties worth $190,000, assume the mortgages against them of approximately $105,000, and take back a first mortgage note of $47,000 for the difference. This would be a 9 percent, 15-year note, with payments of just under $480 a month, and would be placed on the 4-unit property only.

In other words, Mark had traded his three remaining Apple Valley properties for a two-unit property with a $22,000 mortgage against it, and a four-unit property with a $47,000 mortgage against it.

HUD to the Rescue

In order to make this deal work, Mark had to turn the boarded-up six units that were facing condemnation into attractive rental spaces. He did this by taking advantage of a HUD program in his county. The program would match every dollar an owner put into rehabilitating a residential property with a dollar of program funds. These funds would come in the form of a no-interest loan, whose principal would be forgiven at 10 percent a year for ten years as long as the participating owner continued to own the property. In short, the matching funds would be virtually a gift to the owner if he held the property for at least ten years . . . which Mark planned to do.

So Mark put $35,000 of his own money into fixing up the four units, and got free matching funds of $35,000 to make $70,000 worth of improvements.

"I now have a four-unit property worth $175,000 that's in pristine condition," asserts Mark. "It brings in $1,520 per month in rents, and yields a positive cash flow of $900 a month, discounting whatever pay-back value I want to place on the fix-up money I put into it.

"From the two-unit property—which is also in great shape now—I get $875 rent a month. The mortgage payment is $225. Taxes, insurance, and everything else is about $100. So I'm getting about a $550 a month positive cash flow, which is exactly what I would have been *paying* each month for those two vacant lots if I hadn't traded them."

It's Time to Count the Chips

The deal that started with a $20,000 down payment generated in a matter of a few months an approximate $85,000 net, pre-tax, cash profit *plus* three properties that appraised for $190,000, and against which there were $110,000 worth of mortgages. Mark then traded his $80,000 equity in those three properties, plus $47,000 "boot," for six residential units, in which his equity is now close to $170,000, and which produces a combined positive cash flow of roughly $1,450 a month.

But the deal ain't over yet.

One last profitable twist remains to be told. Explains Mark: "Steve Thomas has always taught that any time you write a note, you should stipulate that you have the first right to purchase that note if it is ever offered for sale at a discount. So I put that in the $47,000 mortgage note I wrote to the Laguna Beach investor.

"It wasn't three months later that I got a phone call from a note broker saying, 'I notice that you have the first right to buy this note. This guy's trying to sell it to me. Will you waive your right?'

"I said no. Then I contacted the investor in Laguna Beach. He said he wanted $30,000 for the note. Then I called the note broker back. He said he was going to pay $30,000 for the note, but I showed him that because of the improvements I'd made, it should be worth at least $35,000. He agreed.

"So I called the guy in Laguna Beach back and said, 'Okay, I'll pay you $30,000.' And I called the note broker back and said, 'Okay, I'll sell it to you for $35,000.' The whole thing was in and out of escrow within about 36 hours. I didn't really do anything, but I got a check for $5,000.

"When I think about this whole deal," concludes Mark, "I think of the six Victorville units, the quick $5,000 profit from turning the $47,000 note, and the earlier $85,000 cash profit as all coming from that first purchase of those dumpy Apple Valley properties, which I 'charged' on my credit cards.

"I keep making more and more money on it, and it keeps going on and on and on."

CHAPTER 36

The Trailer Home
That Spawned a Fortune

In 1980 Chris Slater and his wife Ginny moved with their two children into a $50 trailer home in Victoria, British Columbia, Canada.

It had only been two years since the Slaters had moved to Victoria from Edmonton to retire after having achieved uncommon success in real estate and business. Chris was only 31 at the time. But the diamond of prosperity quickly turned to ashes through a series of unfortunate business investments. Chris took a job with a furnace manufacturer, where he would work for ten years. Ginny was a full-time wife and mother, and worked in a series of part-time businesses that met with little success.

By 1980 the Slaters were forced to sell their home and go "back to the land." They purchased 3.96 acres of land in Victoria for $28,000. (All dollar figures mentioned in this chapter are Canadian dollars.) They used their last $14,000 for the down payment and financed the balance. Then they bought a trailer home for $50 and moved in.

Fifty dollars? That amount may sound ridiculously low, but Chris is quick to point out that in this case, seeing is believing. It was in horrible shape. In fact, he had to make some repairs with a chain saw.

"We lived in that trailer for four years with our two young children, a cat, and a guinea pig," he says. "We also had goats, chickens, rabbits, and ducks."

Seedbed of Fortune

Back then, Chris and Ginny could surely not have guessed that their humble home would be the seedbed of a fortune.

The following year, needing more land for his animals, Chris asked his neighbor to the north if he would be willing to sell him some of his property—3.91 acres to be exact. The neighbor said he would . . . for $35,000. "How did you arrive at that figure?" queried Chris. "I just paid $28,000 for mine, and mine has access. Yours has a swamp in the front."

The neighbor held firm, and Chris ended up buying an option to purchase the land for $35,000. The option cost $100. Chris and Ginny then subdivided the total of 7.87 acres into two lots. "Subdividing," in this case, consisted of adjusting the boundaries between the two lots. They created one 5½ acre lot, and another lot just larger than 2¼ acres. They kept the 5½ acres for themselves, and *sold the 2¼ acre lot for $60,000. This yielded a gross profit of $25,000.*

All of this—the exercising of the option, the boundary adjustment, and the sale of the smaller lot—happened simultaneously.

Chris and Ginny used much of the $25,000 windfall to start building their dream home on their land. (Because of other money-hungry investments along the way, this would prove to be a long process. They didn't move in until '85, and were still adding the finishing touches in '91.)

In the Path of Progress

Obviously, land in that area of Victoria was appreciating rapidly. Chris points out that most of the land closer to the center of the city was already developed, and that their land is in the path of growth. Also, Victoria is one of Canada's favorite retirement meccas.

As the value of their land rose, the Slaters were able to borrow against it several times to raise money for other real estate and business investments. Says Chris: "The point of all of this is that by investing in our own home, and having the good fortune of seeing where the path of progress was going, we bought a property that we've been able to refinance many times to fund other investments."

One of those investments cost $11,035, which bought them the distribution rights and inventory of a company called Modern Maintenance Products (MMP). "It seems we're always making money in real estate and losing it on businesses," sighs Chris. This business was no exception. Fourteen months later, Chris and Ginny decided to sell the unprofitable venture to a salesman, Sandy McEwen.

"At the time, Sandy was behind on his house payments as a result of previous unsuccessful employment and business ventures," explains Chris. "We decided to trade the business to him for the down payment, and assume the existing first mortgage of $51,049 (12¼ percent interest) for the balance. We agreed on a price of $62,000 for the house—which was located on Short Street. This meant that the business was worth just under $11,000 to us in trade value."

Because the Short Street house was generating a negative cash flow, Chris immediately began looking for a buyer. He offered it for sale at a monthly meeting of the local real estate investor support group. A young man in the back stood up and said he wanted to buy it. As it turned out, he and his wife were the tenants in the house, whom Sandy had found prior to the sale. His name was Michell. He was a self-employed wood carver. His wife, Rita, was an unemployed financial planner who was going through chemotherapy. They had neither money nor bright prospects—just the dream of owning their own home.

"We really tried to reach a deal with them," says Chris, "but we just couldn't afford to sell them the property on their terms, so we began looking for another buyer."

They soon found a way to trade the Short Street house. An older mansion on Caledonia Street had been converted to a five-unit apartment property. The sales price was $111,500. Chris and Ginny gave the owner their equity in the Short Street house (determined to be $14,000) as a down payment. The balance and the mortgage placement costs were financed by an assumption of an existing first mortgage of $63,643 at 12¾ percent interest, and a new second mortgage of $32,500 at 17¾ percent interest, which was secured by a blanket mortgage on the Slater's personal home and rental properties.

"They skinned us for that second mortgage," quips Chris, "but we really wanted that property."

When the new owner of the Short Street house mentioned to Chris that he wanted to sell it rather than hold it, Chris quickly told him about Michell and Rita. Because the new owner's financial needs were different than the Slater's, they were able to strike a deal. The young couple got their home.

Cash Flow isn't Everything

Mustering the rest of their financial strength, the Slaters borrowed yet another $20,000 against their personal residential lot to do the repairs and renovations necessary to make the Caledonia mansion a first-class property. Even with that, however, the Caledonia generated a slightly negative cash flow overall.

But cash flow isn't everything. After only two and a half years (in January, 1990), Chris and Ginny sold the Caledonia property for $263,000 cash—$151,500 more than what they had paid for it. *Their net profit was over $125,000* after paying the mortgages, renovation expenses, sales commission and closing fees, and the slight negative cash flow costs.

And it all sprang from a piece of land they bought years before to put a $50 trailer home on.

That's not the end of the story. Chris recently received notice from the government that the one-land road running by the land where they are now living in their finished dream home is going to be upgraded to a full highway. Someone is developing 70 lots just to the north of their land. (By the way, Chris and Ginny purchased another 3.37 acres of land from the Crown over a year ago, giving them almost nine acres of land there.)

"My engineers tell me we'll eventually be able to put 35 lots in out there," says Chris. "Those lots will be worth about $70,000 each, when finished. So now we're sitting on *$2.45 million dollars in eventual gross sales!*"

But even that is not the end of the story. For Chris and Ginny, money isn't the final pay-off. When assessing the success of their investment activities, they look for the end results in human terms. One positive result is their own relationship.

"Ginny and I do everything as full partners," Chris points out, "and she's definitely the better half of the partnership. We do everything together. That includes our real estate and business activities. She manages the properties and we're on the titles jointly. She's very skilled in human relations and working effectively with people.''

The Human Side of Real Estate

Other positive human results have spun off from this deal. Sandy McEwen got his own business. Michell and Rita got their own home—a house which has skyrocketed in value since they purchased it. (They were offered $125,000 for it in '89.)

Not long ago Chris was at a grocery store when a disfigured woman limped over to him and grabbed his arm. She appeared to be elderly. ''I have to talk to you,'' she said. Chris did not recognize her. ''It's Rita,'' she continued. ''Nobody recognizes me anymore, but I've wanted to thank you for a long time for helping Michell and me get into our own home.''

Her eyes clouded with tears. ''It was always our dream to have our own home, and you helped make it come true. Now we have memories we'll always treasure. God bless you.''

With that, she walked away. To this day, Chris considers her words of gratitude to be the deal's biggest pay-off.

CHAPTER 37

A Mobile Investor and Her Mobile Home

In April of 1990, Gayle Langland was pulling her car into the parking lot of a hardware store in the desert town of Indio, California, when she saw an elderly lady walking out of the store carrying a "For Sale" sign. The sight triggered a flag in her mind that read, "Opportunity!"

"I was with my partner," explains Gayle. "She always jokes that I shoved her out the door to run and ask the lady what she was selling because I wasn't even parked yet and she was about to get into her car and drive off."

As it turned out, the elderly lady was indeed elderly—85 years old, to be exact—and was quite a real estate investor in her own right. In fact, she had had a younger woman drive her to California from her home in Salt Lake City to sell her trailer home in Indio. Why did she want to sell it? Because her investment activities had kept her so busy recently that she hadn't been able to "winter out" in sunny Southern California as she usually did. And she was too much of a business woman to bring herself to go on paying the monthly trailer park fees when she was too busy at home to get her money out of them.

A Week to Sell

So she was buying a "For Sale" sign. And she was going to sell the

170

home before she returned to Salt Lake City within the week.

Recalls Gayle: "Just as someone would say 'Tomorrow's Wednesday,' she said 'I came down to sell it this week.' The way she talked, it was obvious that the thought hadn't even crossed her mind that it might take her longer to sell it."

The 24' by 48' (double-wide) mobile home was located in a trailer park called Bermuda Palms Mobile Estates. Gayle told the lady she was interested in possibly purchasing it. She went to see it that evening.

The home was 30 years old and a mess, but was very well made. It was a one-bedroom trailer with a fairly large kitchen, a dining room, a large living room, and a sun porch. The lady had owned it for about 15 years, had purchased it for $18,000, and now wanted at least $15,000 for it.

"We began that night by looking around the park to see what else was for sale," recalls Gayle. "And the next day we made some calls and went to see some others that were for sale. We also called a mobile home dealer and went to see some mobile homes in other parks. Based on what we could buy that would be comparable and didn't need all the digging out and cleaning up, we decided that $15,000 was too much. Also, we couldn't pay that at that time, because she wanted cash.

"We could have bought one in perfect move-in condition that wasn't quite as big for $13,000. So based on what we saw, I decided to make a lowball offer. I didn't know how she'd take it. I didn't want to insult her or be unkind. I said, 'I don't want to insult you, but I feel that based on what we've looked at and what we can afford to pay, $10,000 is the most we can offer.' I didn't say anything about cash, although I was prepared to pay cash. She said she'd have to think about it."

Fast Work

Gayle made this offer the day after she met the elderly lady at the hardware store. This was fast work because the mobile homeowner was not the only one who was an "out-of-towner" and needed to get home to take care of business. Gayle, too, was a visitor. She had only come to Indio to take care of some business. She lived in Idyllwild, an hour's drive away up into the mountains.

However, Gayle and her partner made frequent trips to Indio. Their real estate investments had increasingly brought them out of the mountains and into the desert area in and around Indio. They had, in fact, been keeping their eyes open for a property they could use as a combined office and residence when they were in the area, rather than stay in motels. Nevertheless, Gayle was pursing this trailer home purchase with the idea of fixing it up and selling it for profit.

The day after Gayle made the offer, the elderly lady called and said she would accept the offer. Gayle went over immediately to make sure she knew what she was buying. But before they had a chance to talk about how the $10,000 would be paid, the owner discovered that she couldn't find the deed to the home or any of the papers.

Because of this, Gayle suggested that she pay her a $5,000 cash down payment and put the other $5,000 cash on a note at 10 percent interest that would be payable in six months. In the meantime, the lady could find the deed.

Both parties agreed to these arrangements. Within a few weeks, Gayle and her partner got access to the mobile home and made a big push to get it fixed up and renovated before the hottest weather hit in late June or early July. With the help of a couple they brought in from Idyllwild, they finished most of the work within three weeks.

"It was really dirty," recalls Gayle. "We took about five loads of stuff to the dump, and had to have the kitchen dug out. The knobs on the kitchen cabinets were so dirty we had to replace them. We replaced the carpeting and curtains and did the usual fix-up work. And we worked on the lot, which is quite nice. Even after we got the place into fairly good condition in the first two to three weeks, we continued to make improvements here and there afterwards. All in all, we spent about $5,000 on improvements and fix-up."

Gayle didn't want to be in Indio during the summer months, so she rented the mobile home to a real estate friend for $350 a month plus utility costs. This was a lower rent than she could have charged. But even with the park fee of $240 a month (which included taxes), and the insurance cost of about $23 a month, she still made a positive monthly cash flow of over $80.

Had she been making mortgage payments on a $10,000 loan, however, that positive cash flow would have been negative.

The renter stayed in the mobile home not only through the summer, but through the fall and most of the winter as well—until

February, 1991.

A Year's Closing

Getting the paperwork done on the deal was a hassle. Gayle would ask for certain documents, and the elderly lady would send her the wrong papers. It took more than a year after they arranged the sale to get everything finished. Gayle's portion of the closing costs totaled less than $500.

"We told her that because the deal took so long to close," says Gayle, "we felt that we shouldn't have to pay interest on the $5,000 note." She said that was fair.

The second $5,000 payment, like the first, was basically an out-of-pocket expense. Gayle had checked on borrowing the money, but it looked as if it would have been more trouble than it was worth.

When the renter moved out of the mobile home in February, Gayle and her partner decided that they would use it as a satellite office and a residence when they were in Indio. They found that it lent itself well to both these functions.

Thanks to their "sweat equity," Gayle figures that the mobile home is now worth between $20,000 and $22,000. This represents a 33 to 47 percent appreciation factor in just over a year.

But the mobile home's true value is as a residence and office for Gayle and her partner. For an investment of about $15,000, Gayle has acquired an asset that has rapidly appreciated and is saving her hundreds of dollars each month in satellite office/residence costs for her Indio investment activities.

One Last Benefit

Gayle loves having a second home in Indio. With only an hour's drive between her mountain home and her desert retreat, she can quickly and easily position herself to fully enjoy all the cool summers and warm winters the two areas have to offer.

CHAPTER 38

Snatching Profits from the Jaws of Foreclosure

"In 1985 the big thing around here was to buy properties just before they went into foreclosure," explains Sue Brawn, real estate investor from Dayton, Ohio. "My partner, Earl Lang (also known as 'Sir Handy') found a series of properties owned by the same person that were in pre-foreclosure in Miamisburg, Ohio."

One was an old seven-unit building. Another was a two-unit apartment. There were also two houses. But the property that most captivated Sue was a brick commercial building that housed a pizza place that was going out of business, a carry-out that was hanging on by its teeth, and two 3-bedroom, 1400 square-foot apartments upstairs. The building was located on a corner right out of downtown Miamisburg where the main bridge is located. It sat on 1.2 acres of land, but much of that was on a hill.

"This property particularly interested us because it had the potential of becoming an office building," says Sue. "We own a company called Tenant Chek, and were looking for a larger space for our operation."

The Biggest Mess in the World

The seller wanted $155,000 for the corner building. Even though that was what it appraised for, Sue didn't think it was worth that. So she made an offer of $90,000 in pre-foreclosure. "He liked that," she states, "so we went and talked to his attorney, and got involved in the biggest mess in the world. We couldn't get the property out of foreclosure even though the savings and loan that held the mortgage was willing to have us buy it. The whole series of properties finally went into foreclosure.

"The city condemned the old seven-unit building and we decided not to try to get it. Someone else got it, but hadn't done his homework, and the city tore it down. One of the houses and the two-unit apartment building went up for foreclosure, but we passed on those, too, because we discovered they weren't well-made.

"But I *lusted* after that corner office building and the house behind it on the hill, which was now a separate package."

At the foreclosure sale, several people bid on the building, but not enough to cover the outstanding mortgage balance owed to the savings and loan.

This Bud's for You

By this point—winter of 1986—the pizza house and carry-out business were gone. The tenants in the two upstairs apartments were not paying rent. It was a cold winter. Sue was ready to make her move. She had done her homework, and had talked to the people at the savings and loan that held the mortgage. Having done business with her before, they were more than willing to help her take it off their hands.

She offered $58,000.

Says Sue: "I talked the S&L into giving us what I call a 'Bud' loan. Bud was the president of the S&L. I got an adjustable-rate loan for the *full $58,000* for 20 years at 9¼ percent interest. And believe it or not, they gave me a six-month moratorium on payments! Plus, they gave me a loan to fix up the building for $10,000 at 10 percent interest, renewable yearly, with interest-only payments. We bought the place in January, 1987.

"We went in and did everything we could. My partner Earl rehabbed the old pizza house for less than $1,000. Of course, that doesn't include our labor. We turned it into a very beautiful office for Tenant

Chek with a reception area, storage area, a room where we screen tenants, and a large private office.''

To make a long story short, the entire building was soon renovated. The non-paying tenants in the two upstairs apartments were evicted and replaced. The side of the downstairs that housed the carry-out operation was converted to three attractive offices and rented out. The building is now considered to be a credit to the community.

A Healthy Appreciation

Best of all, it's *now worth approximately $200,000*—a far cry from the $58,000 purchase price Sue negotiated early in '87. Future appreciation looks very healthy, too. The bridge in front of the building is in the final stages of being rebuilt, so the property will be the first thing to be seen by the increased traffic that will be entering town from that direction. Also, Sue and Earl continue forcing appreciation by making further improvements inside and out.

With the small mortgage amount, it is not surprising that the property generates a positive cash flow. In fact, Sue says that *the monthly cash flow runs between $350 and $400.* This is in spite of the fact that a good portion of the building is being used for Sue's business.

By the way, what happened to the house behind the office building that Sue also wanted to buy? She and her partner bought that, too, in a separate transaction.

But that's another story.

CHAPTER 39

Keeping His Options Open

 " **A** real estate broker called me in 1984," recounts Bob Bruss, San Francisco Bay area investor, "and said he had an out-of-town owner who wanted to lease a house and get a steady monthly income of $500 with no headaches."

The two-story, three-bedroom house, located in a nice residential area in Pacifica, was worth $125,000 at the time.

"After he described it, I said, 'Fine, I'll lease the house, but I want an option to buy it.' So we wrote up a 15-year lease option at $500 a month net to the owner. I would send the owner $500 a month, make a $350 monthly payment on an existing first mortgage on the house, take care of all the maintenance, pay the property taxes, and so on.

"I would also have the right to sublease to a tenant. And I could buy the house (subject to the existing mortgage) at any time within the next 15 years by paying the owner $100,000 for his equity. Of course, I would also have to pay off or assume the mortgage balance at the time I exercised the option."

Reaping the Benefits of Equity Build-up

Because the mortgage balance was about $25,000, and was fairly new, this was basically the same as a $125,000 option. By structuring it the way he did, however, Bob reaps the benefits of the equity build-up as the mortgage is paid down.

The owner lived out of town. *Way* out of town. In Sri Lanka (formerly Ceylon), to be exact. He had retired there where the living was cheap and good. He lived like a king, with a home, two servants . . . the works. Five hundred dollars a month was more than he needed.

Bob met with him to finalize the deal when he was in town for a few days. "The question of what I was going to give him up front came up," recalls Bob. "I thought real fast and said, 'Well, why don't I pay you a year's rent in advance?' That was $6,000. Also, I thought I should pay him something for the 15-year option, so I paid him the grand sum of $1.

"We also negotiated a rent credit to be applied to the $100,000 for part of the monthly $500 lease payments. I originally wanted a 50 percent credit, but somehow he got me down to 17 percent. (Don't ask me where that figure came from.) Every time I pay him the 1500 lease payment, the original $100,000 is reduced by another $85."

It was decided that the real estate agent would get a $6,000 commission for his part in the deal, and that Bob would pay him half of that up front, and the other $3,000 when he exercised the option. "Every time I see that agent," laughs Bob, "he says, 'Hey, I think today would be a great time to exercise your option!' "

Bob took control of the Pacifica house. The same tenant has been in the house the entire time, and the rent has gradually increased to its current level of $1,000 a month.

At the first of each year, Bob sends the owner twelve postdated checks for $500 each for his monthly lease payments. He also sends the $25,000 mortgage holder the $350 mortgage payment each month *directly*. ("You should always do this when you have a lease option to make sure it gets paid," Bob suggests. "In this case, the owner wrote the mortgage holder a letter saying that I would be managing the house and they would receive payments from me.")

Good News, Bad News

With those payments and all other expenses, Bob's cash flow on the property has been roughly a break-even situation.

That's the bad news . . . or at least the not-so-great news. The good news is that *the home, just seven years later, is wroth $225,000 at the minimum.* That's about $132,000 more than the approximate $93,000 that it would cost Bob to exercise his option and buy it ($100,000 minus the rent credits, which now total over $7,000). Of course, he would have to either pay off the original $25,000 mortgage or continue making $350 monthly payments on it until completely amortized, which is still a few years down the road.

"It has been a great investment," states Bob.

But something happened recently that promised to make it even better . . . better for Bob, at least.

The owner died in February, 1991. (It's safe to assume that he died a happy man in his tropical paradise.) Bob explains: "His two brothers inherited his estate. There isn't much in his estate other than this house. They really want me to exercise the option because they want to get the estate settled and out of the way.

"Of course, I'm saying 'Well, there are about eight years left on the 15-year option. I'm in no hurry. But, if you'll give me a big enough discount off the less than $93,000 it would take to exercise my option, I would be glad to exercise it now instead of waiting another eight years.'

A Solid Gold Investment

Bob is currently negotiating the discount price with the brothers. It will be somewhere *between $50,000 and $75,000!* For a $225,000 home—a house whose rental income has paid its own lease payments and all other expenses, and will have finished paying off the $25,000 mortgage in a few years—that would have to be considered a solid gold investment in anyone's book.

In short, Bob will have purchased a $225,000 home for between $50,000 and $75,000. Since rental income has paid for everything else, his only other real expense in the property is the $6,000 broker's commission. His profit on the deal, then, will be *between $144,000 and $169,000.*

Not bad for a $1 option!

CHAPTER 40

The Little House that Became a Big Money Machine

There's an old vaudeville gag that goes something like this. Fred: "Say, Joe, I hear you won a big contest. What's the first prize?" Joe: "A trip to Pittsburgh." Fred: "Really? What's the second prize?" Joe: "*Two* trips to Pittsburgh." (General laughter.)

Pittsburgh has changed for the better since the golden days of vaudeville. That joke wouldn't fly today. Too many people think the Pennsylvania metropolis is an all-around nice place to visit and to live.

Jean Yevick is one of those people. She likes living there. And she *really* likes investing in real estate there.

Ready for Renovation

Her favorite real estate deal involves a gutted house that she bought in 1980 for $9,600 cash. The home was located a short distance from her own residence in Pittsburgh. It was a four-story house on a steep hill, with two floors above street level and two below. The owner had just gutted it and was ready to renovate it when he got a job transfer and had to move. He wanted $13,000.

Jean saw the ad in the newspaper and after inspecting it, offered $9,600 cash. Another potential buyer offered more, but wanted the owner to carry a mortgage for part of the amount. Jean's offer was accepted. She bought the home in February of 1980.

She knew she had made a good deal—especially when she added up the value of what the seller had left behind, including glass sliding doors, a water heater, and other items worth close to $5,000!

Jean's attorney, smelling a good deal, asked if he could be her partner on the deal. She said yes, and they both wrote checks for $4,800.

Jean's plan was to convert the gutted home into a shipshape, attractive, two-unit residential property. There would be a two-bedroom apartment and a one-bedroom apartment.

"The house was in the city," says Jean, "so urban redevelopment money was available. These were government funds administered through the city. I was able to get an $18,000 grant to fix up the property. As long as I complied with the rules and kept the property for five years, I wouldn't have to pay that money back. It would be free. And the rules weren't very restrictive."

While they were waiting for the redevelopment funds—which took over six months to arrive—Jean's attorney decided he wanted to get out of the deal. She bought him out, paying him the $4,800 he had put into it.

Thinking that she would need $33,000 to accomplish her goals for the home, Jean borrowed another $15,000 from a bank to supplement the $18,000 redevelopment grant. This was a 15-year, 12 percent interest first mortgage loan, with monthly payments of $180. "But I didn't have to make payments on all that money right away," she explains. "I drew on it as we did the project, and we were able to use the $18,000 grant money first. So I didn't have to make any mortgage payments until the project was almost finished. I didn't draw a dollar of the $15,000 loan for about four months."

A Windfall Cut

It was early in '82 before the remodeling was finished and ready for occupancy. The project had put the property in mint condition, with a new roof, good insulation, new siding, new mechanical equipment, and so on.

"The contractor was able to bring it in for $28,000—$5,000 less than what I had planned on," says Jean. *"That $5,000 went into my pocket,* because the loan was for $15,000 and the grant was for $18,000, and there was no way that we could change those numbers."

The $5,000 windfall cut in half the out-of-pocket investment Jean had put into the property (the $9,600 cash purchase price plus miscellaneous expenses). Her total investment was now approximately $5,000, and she had a newly remodeled two-unit rental property with only a $15,000 mortgage loan against it.

In 1983, Jean decided to refinance. She went through a finance company. "The appraisal came in at $33,000, which was ridiculously low," she points out. "But the loan proceedings had dragged on so long that by the time they were ready to close I had to take it because I didn't have time to go elsewhere for it. I had already committed the money I was planning to take out of the deal."

The $33,000 appraisal permitted Jean to borrow $23,000, which she did. With that $23,000, she paid off the earlier $15,000 mortgage loan and all closing costs. *This left $6,100 on the table for her.*

Since she had previously reimbursed herself for $5,000 of her total out-of-pocket investment on the deal, this additional $6,100 paid back the rest of it and gave her over $1,000 to boot. Her monthly payments on the new mortgage were $300. Her gross monthly rental income from the two apartments was $550. The tenants paid all their own utilities. Taxes and insurance expenses ran $43 per month. (Because the property was on the government grant program, the taxes couldn't be raised during the five-year period.) So *her cash flow was positive—over $200 a month!*

Praise for the Appraiser

Because she knew that the $33,000 appraisal was way below what it should have been, Jean refinanced the loan once again just six months later, in January 1984. This time she went through a regular bank, and a qualified MAI appraiser pegged the home's value at $53,000, a full $20,000 higher than the other appraisal had been!

Jean could have borrowed up to 80 percent of the appraised value, but elected to borrow only $39,500 in order to maintain a positive cash flow. This was a 15-year mortgage note, with monthly payments of close to $440.

With the $39,500 loan proceeds, Jean paid off the existing $23,000 mortgage and all closing costs. *"Then I walked away with the balance, which was about $13,000,"* she states.

After pocketing the $13,000, *Jean had taken a total of over $14,000 out of the property in cash.* Incredibly, even with winnings of that magnitude from a small property, it was still producing a positive monthly cash flow. The rental income by then was $590 a month. With monthly mortgage payments of about $440 and tax and insurance expenses of close to $45, Jean was the happy recipient of an approximate $105 positive monthly cash flow.

"I didn't need the money then," explains Jean, "so I put it back into the mortgage payments each month. In the early years of a mortgage, most of the money you pay is interest. By using my cash flow to reduce the principal balance each month, it started coming down pretty fast."

Stretching the Payments

As the property's rental income increased during the coming years, the cash flow grew, and Jean continued plowing it all back into accelerated principal payments on the mortgage. When, after about five years, the principal balance had been chiseled down to just over $24,500, she went to the bank that held the mortgage and said, "I'm paying $440 a month, and I only owe about $24,500 at this point in time. How much would you charge me to redo the loan? I don't want to take any cash out. I just want you to redo it for 15 more years to stretch it out again and get a lower monthly payment."

The charges were about $200, and the new 15-year, 11.5 percent interest loan was written up and signed. This lowered the new mortgage payment to $288 a month. Sometimes, when Jean has extra money, she uses it to pay down the principal balance, but does this only on a "when convenient" basis.

Today, the mortgage balance has been paid to $22,500. The rental income is $675 per month, and she has no problem keeping the two units occupied. The mortgage payment is $288. Taxes run $75 a month, and insurance, $18 a month. The home is still in top condition, so maintenance expenses are nil. The tenants pay all other costs. Jean's current positive monthly cash flow on the property is $294.

The value of the property, due to local real estate trends, remains close to the $53,000 level for which it appraised in '84.

A Growing Equity

Summing up, Jean had very little of her own money into this deal in the first place—and only had it in for three years. Since then, *the property has put more than $14,000 in cash into her pocket, plus well over $10,000 in positive cash flow.* Beyond all this, she owns a property worth roughly $53,000, and against which there is only $22,500 in debt. *That makes her equity $30,500.* Best of all, that equity will grow every month.

Her plans for the two-unit rental house? "I've thought about selling it and pocketing the cash, or holding the financing," she reflects. "But I didn't want to because of the capital gains situation. Also—I'll have to admit—it produces such a great cash flow and has been such a low-maintenance property that I'd hate to sell it now."

CHAPTER 41

A Profitable
Dinner Conversation

Here's the story:
The year of 1981 was the peak
and final burst of a long, oil-fed boom in
Alberta, Canada. A builder, riding the
wave of the economic euphoria, built 44
condominium townhouses in Morinville, a
little town outside Alberta.

Looking for a profitable place to put his money, a physician purchased 20 of the 44 units. He paid $55,000 per unit, and borrowed
about $40,000 against each one in separate mortgage notes from the
same institutional lender.

Unfortunately, his timing was off. The closing took place on the
last day of the 10-year boom. Nevertheless, he kept the properties,
had a manager run them, and did fine with them for the next five
years—until 1986. In fact, he made a positive cash flow.

In 1986, the mortgage came up for renewal. "This is one of the
differences between Canadian financing and United States
financing," explains Raymond Aaron, Toronto real estate investor
and educator. "Whereas the amortization period in the United States
is typically 30 years, and the term is also 30 years, in Canads, the
amortization period is typically 25 years, and the term is typically one
to five years. There's no such thing as a 25- to 30-year mortgage. It
doesn't exist in Canada."

In short, Canadian mortgages are somewhat similar to United States mortgages that have one- to three-year balloons. In Canada, unless there are unusual circumstances, it's almost a foregone conclusion that the mortgage will be renewed for another term at an updated interest rate.

Gave Back the Keys

In the case of the good doctor and his 20 condominiums, there were unusual circumstances. Because five years of bad times had transpired since he had bought the townhouses at their peak price of $55,000, and especially because the value of the condos had fallen to $29,000 during that period, the lender refused to renew the mortgages. So the doctor did the manly thing: he handed them the keys and told them to look him up if they ever needed quality proctology work. (After all, turnabout is fair play.)

The lender started calling real estate brokers but couldn't find one to list the units. They were only asking $29,000 for each of the three-bedroom, two-story, fully carpeted, fully renovated townhouses. Still, no one would even list them, so deep was the local depression.

"They finally dropped the price to $25,000 in order to get a listing," says Raymond. "Even at that price, the townhouses sat there until late 1987 without getting any offers. They were renting for about $400 a month and the tenants were paying all utilities.

The Bank is Willing

"I found out about the deal in November of '87, and I agreed to buy the whole lot. I got on the phone and said, 'I'll offer you $23,000 but no more.' I would have paid $25,000. They said, 'Fine,' All they wanted was to have a closing on December 31, because if it closed by then, it would be off their books.

"Then I said, 'You've got to give me 80 percent mortgages on each of the townhouses.' They pointed out that the Bank Act of Canada prohibits banks from giving more than 75 percent mortgages on properties unless they're mortgage-insured. So I said, 'Okay, forget the deal,' and they said, 'Okay, it's 80 percent.'

"Then I told them I wanted 10 percent interest and they told me that wasn't their rate. So I said, 'Okay, forget the deal,' and they said, 'Ten percent it is.' Then I said I wanted to fully open (that is, I could pay it off at any time without penalty), and they said they wouldn't be able to do that. So I said, 'Well, let's forget the deal,' and they said, 'All right, it's fully open.'

"I then said, 'Look, I want you to guarantee that all 20 units are rented on the date of closing.' They said fine. I said, 'I want you to guarantee that all appliances in all 20 units are in perfect condition on the date of closing.' They said, 'Fine, what else do you want?' I was just about to ask them to shampoo the carpets, but I realized, 'Hey, the deal's good enough. I don't need to push it.' "

Raymond continued to ask for this and that, and each time, the lender said "Fine, but do you *promise* you'll still close on December 31?"

Food for Thought

Still Raymond had to come up with the 20 percent down payment—a mere $92,000. He was planning to come up with all of it himself, but at a dinner at which he was asked to speak, something interesting happened. "I was sitting with my mortgage broker and my lawyer," he recalls. "We were the guests of honor, and were each supposed to give a speech at this special convention, so we were sitting at the table together.

"They always ask me what I'm doing. So I said I had just bought 20 very nice, fully rented townhouses at $23,000 apiece. Their jaws fell open. When I said I had to come up with $92,000, and that I was just going to cut a check for it, my lawyer said, 'How about me?' And I said, 'How *about* you?'

"If I come up with the down payment, can I have half the deal?" asked the lawyer.

When Raymond said, "Why not?" the attorney pulled out his checkbook and began to write out a check for $92,000. Then the mortgage broker said, "What about me?"

"I own half the property now," said the lawyer. "You can have half of my half if you write me a check for forty-six."

With that, the mortgage broker pulled out *his* checkbook and started writing a check. When he came to the amount, he looked up and said, "By the way, is that forty-six *hundred* or forty-six *thousand*?" The lawyer said, "Forty-six *thousand.*"

"Oh, okay," replied the mortgage broker casually.

He didn't even know the details of the deal," laughs Raymond. "He just knew it was good. Of course, the people sitting around us couldn't believe all this was happening. So there I am sitting at the table waiting to speak, and my lawyer on my left side gives me a check for $46,000 and my mortgage broker on my right side gives me another check for $46,000. I put them both in my wallet, and got up to give my speech."

The closing took place on December 31, 1987. Raymond bought the 20 townhouses for $23,000 apiece. The lender/owner gave him 10 percent interest mortages for 80 percent of that amount, amortized over a 25-year period, with five-year terms.

At the closing, the attorney and the lawyer paid for all the closing costs that accrued to the buyers. In short, Raymond was into a major deal without a penny of his own money. He owned a 50 percent interest, and his two partners each held 25 percent interests.

Cashing in for Profits

Raymond had agreed that he would cash out either the attorney or the mortgage broker, or both, if at any time they wanted out of the deal. For three years, they owned the properties together, making a positive cash flow, which they plowed back into capital improvements on the units. All in all, over the three years, their overall cash flow was a negative $2,000, which works out to be $2.78 per unit per month.

Late in '90, Raymond's two partners decided they wanted to sell the properties. The area was in the midst of a recession and things were a bit tight. Raymond said he'd get them listed.

"I phoned a local real estate agent," he relates. "He said, 'I don't think you could get a penny over $43,000 for those properties,' I said, 'Great.' We listed with him, and within about a month, he sold them all to different people for $43,000 each."

It's calculator time. "Forty-three thousand dollars minus $23,000 is $20,000 a door; times 20 doors is $400,000," figures Raymond. "Half of that is mine: $200,000. A quarter of it went to each of the other two investors: $100,000. They got their $46,000 apiece back, plus $100,000 each. They did no work whatsoever. They had no worries. They had no problems. With their original down payment and principal paydown over the three years, which were offset basically by the expenses of the sales commissions and closing costs, they got their money back plus about a 200 percent profit in three years."

Raymond's profit is easier to calculate. Since he put nothing into the deal, a return of even $1 would have made his return infinite. That's the beauty of the no-down deal.

Consider the other $199,999 as frosting on the cake.

CHAPTER 42

The Church Connection

" **A** 3½ bedroom home built around 1890 had been occupied by an elderly woman who was a member of our church," explains James Koski, real estate investor from Saginaw, Michigan. "She was an only child, had been born on the kitchen table in the house, and had lived in it all her life. Until the last 30 years, her father had lived there with her. She had set things up in her estate in a way that the church would get the house when she died or became incapacitated and had to be put in a rest home."

In 1989, when she was 93, the latter occurrence took place. The church was given the property, but wasn't equipped to assume the responsibility of taking care of it. Knowing that James bought properties, the minister contacted him and asked if he'd be interested in taking it off their hands.

James went over to inspect the home. "It was in rough shape," he recalls. "It looked like it hadn't been decorated, painted, or even given a thorough cleaning in 30 years. And although it was livable, it wouldn't have measured up to the local codes for rentals because it needed some plumbing, electrical, and other sorts of work.

Sweating It Out

"I made the church an offer of $8,500, with $8,250 in a land contract, and $250 down. It was an 11 percent interest, six-year contract with monthly payments of $184. There were no closing costs. Since it didn't meet the codes for rentals, I could have had the work done, but that was Plan B. Plan A was to flip it on another contract to someone else who wanted a house to live in and would be willing to go in and pour some sweat equity into it."

The object of the game, at that point, was to find someone who fit that description. The daughter of an acquaintance of James'—a single mother of three on social assistance—fit the bill perfectly.

"I offered it to her for $24,000 with no down payment," he recalls. "Her payments were set at $300 per month which included her taxes and insurance. That was about $50 dollars less than what she had been paying to rent an apartment. In her case, because of her restricted income, that payment will remain the same even when taxes and insurance go up, unless her financial situation changes.

"We wrote another land contract at 11 percent interest, with a 30-year term. By the way 11 percent is the maximum interest rate that can be charged on land contracts in Michigan. That hasn't changed in the last 50 years, at least that I'm aware of."

In short, James purchased a home for $250 and $184 monthly payments for six years. He turned around and sold it for 30 years' worth of $300 monthly payments (from which taxes and insurance would be paid, amounting to a total of about $50 a month). That means he would net approximately $55 per month.

Leaving it right there, this would qualify as a happy ending to an extremely easy, inexpensive, no-hassle deal. But that's not the end of the story. It gets better.

Doing an Extra Step

"I went to my credit union," James explains, "refinanced the property, paid off the church, and put $3,500 in my pocket. I did this by mortgaging the property for $12,000. With that money, I paid the church the balance on the land contract of $8,250 (for which the church gave me the deed to the property), paid myself back the $250 I put into the down payment, and pocketed the remaining $3,500."

The monthly payment on the 10 percent interest, ten-year refinancing loan is about $150. This means that James is paying $34 per month less than before, and although he'll be making those payments for four years longer than if he hadn't refinanced, he now has $3,500 more to play with than if he hadn't pushed the deal the extra step.

The foundation of the deal was buying low and selling for a good price. "I was able to buy at a low price," says James, "because the church was a *don't-wanter*. It's in the business of saving souls—not property."

Happy All Around

James did a bit of soul-saving in this deal himself . . . at least in the material sense. He was able to take a problem off the church's hands. And he helped the young single mother, even though he sold her the house for a relatively high price. "This lady was on welfare," he points out. She had no possibility whatsoever of ever buying a house under normal circumstances. Although I didn't give her a low price, I *did* give her very attractive terms—terms that fit her budget and her situation. It was a good deal for her."

Clearly, it was a good deal for everyone involved.

CHAPTER 43

"The Paper Caper"

It began in 1980, and was destined to become known as "The Paper Caper."

"It was the best single idea that I've ever come up with in terms of making money related to real estate and using mortgages," states Don Tauscher, entrepreneur from Orlando, Florida. "I've done many, many transactions, and they all follow the same basic pattern."

Don set the wheels in motion for "The Paper Caper" by talking to the installment loan vice president at a local bank with whom he had already done business. "He was unknowledgeable in the area of mortgages. I had to educate him thoroughly over the course of several months. We went to about four lunches. Actually, what I did was give him a long seminar. The key to this whole thing was that my personal relationship with the banker was solid, so while he didn't understand what I was doing (and never did), he believed that *I* understood, and that credibility allowed me to do what I did."

And What Was It He Did?

In his own words: "I would contract to buy mortgages held by individuals who had sold properties and carried back mortgage notes—either firsts, or seconds, or wraps—without putting up any money on the front end. I would contract to buy them for, say, 25 percent yields. Then I would take my contracts to the bank and borrow against a closed transaction of assigning those mortgages to the bank, say, at the current rate, which might be perhaps 12 percent. This would all happen in one closing: the purchase of the mortgage and the assignment of the same mortgage to the bank.

"If I could take these pieces of paper to the bank in which I had, say, 25 percent yields, and borrow against them at 18 percent, and pick up the spread on the front end, I would walk away with untaxed cash in my hands because it was borrowed money. (The actual taxable event takes place over the life of the loan, where the interest that's received on the mortgage and the discount portion for the particular year is taxable in that year.) I also had all my cash up front.

"We did all these transactions by assignment so that I would stay in ownership and use the mortgage paper just like a stock certificate or car title, to borrow against."

A Line of Credit

Obviously, Don needed money to buy the mortgages in the first place. That's where the banker came in. He arranged to give Don a $250,000 line of credit to be used to carry out his plans to buy mortgage paper. Getting this $250,000 credit line (which was raised within a relatively short time to $500,000) was actually Don's "best deal." It was this deal that allowed him to pull off many, many paper caper transactions in the ensuing years.

"The best deal I ever did," states Don, "was establishing this process of banking mortgage notes."

Certain restrictions were placed on borrowing against the line of credit, however. For starters, there was a 75 to 80 percent loan-to-value ratio maximum. That is, the total financing on a property—*all* mortgages against it—could not exceed 75 to 80 percent of its value. Also, the mortgages had to be on single-family residences. (This rule was eventually loosened to permit a broader range of residential property types.) Finally, Don would be listed on the notes as a guarantor.

"In reality," Don points out, "these deals were nothing different than second mortgage loan deals from the bank's risk standpoint.

The bank had the security of the value of the property, plus the person who was making payments on the mortgage and myself to look to if anything went wrong. So the bank's risk was minimal.''

Necessary Paperwork

There was yet another risk-reducer for the bank. Five percent of every loan Don borrowed was placed in a non-interest bearing reserve account. This account would be available to be tapped in case someone was slow or fell behind in making a payment. This would protect the bank, and would protect Don from having to come up with the money to cover the payment out of his pocket. It would also give him the time to collect the money or start foreclosure proceedings.

The bank insisted on an appraisal, too. At first, it insisted on certified appraisals, which cost a few hundred dollars. Don eventually persuaded the bank to accept a sales contract as a verification of value if it was no more than a year old. Finally, Don got the bank's approval to make the appraisal process even easier, and merely get an appraisal in the form of a wholesale purchase offer letter from an investor in the community where the mortgaged house was located.

Other necessary paperwork on each deal included a survey, a credit report on the mortgage owner that would be making the payments, an assignment from the mortgage owner to Don, and then a reassignment to the bank. Also, a security agreement was always involved which stated that the mortgage was not being purchased by the bank, but was security for the loan. This was important in the event of a tax audit. Without the security agreement, the IRS would likely consider the transaction a sale rather than a secured loan.

Closings took about 20 minutes.

Having the cash to buy the mortgages was only part of the equation, however. Don also had to find the mortgages to buy. To do this, he announced to the various real estae organizations to which he belonged that he was buying paper; he spoke to builders and developers who might have carried back seconds on projects; and he ran an ad in the local newspaper, *The Orlando Sentinel*. It read, "I buy mortgages. Call me last." (He also listed his phone number, of course.) This was his most effective mortgage-finder.

Walking Through a Deal

To understand how the theory of this process transaltes to reality, it will be helpful to walk through one of Don's paper caper transactions.

"This particular deal," recalls Don, "involves a new second mortgage on a house. The house sold for $50,000. The buyer assumed a first mortgage of $20,000 and paid $10,000 down. This left $20,000 that the seller carried back in a ten-year second mortgage, with a 12 percent interest rate, and monthly payments of $286.94. This second mortgage is what I bought. I bought it at a yield of 25 percent, which made the price $12,613.14. That's what I contracted to pay for the mortgage at the closing. (Yield is different than discount. Yield is interest rate plus discount, related to the time in which you receive it.)

"I took this second mortgage to the bank and said 'I have contracted to buy an income stream of $286.94 for 120 months. How much would you loan me on it?' Based on our prior arrangements, the banker took his calculator out and said, 'We will loan you $15,924.73.'

"At the closing, I paid the seller of the note $12,613.14, I received a loan against that note from the bank for $15,924.73, which means I walked away from the closing with a $3,311.59 spread, less loan costs of about $125 and the 5 percent reserve of $796. *That left me with $2,390.59 cash.*

It is important to note that Don architected the monthly payments in a way that they would be a "wash" to him. The payments coming in on the $20,000 second mortgage were $286.94 per month. Don's payments to the bank were for that same amount. "You see," says Don, "I matched the payments so they would be a wash. The person making the payments sent them right to the bank. From the closing on, I was out of it.

"This is the way I always do it. I have nothing more to do with the deal unless a payment goes past due, or unless the person pays off early, which is nice, since his payoff with me is greater in most cases than what I owe the bank, so I walk away with more cash."

Selling an Idea

Although the numbers change with each deal, the basic formula remains the same, whether a bank or another money source is used. Don always tries to make at least $1,000 per deal, and has made as much as $18,000.

One of the nice things about the paper caper is that it's counter-cyclical. In recession times, more paper is available than in good times.

Don points out that he has never lost a penny on any paper caper transaction. And it all started with his "best deal": not buying and selling a piece of real estate, but selling a banker on an idea, which enabled him to buy dozens of real estate-backed mortgages.

The Deal That Anybody Could Have Done

Once upon a time—in the spring of '87, to be exact—there was a three-bedroom, single-family home in Romeoville, Illinois about a half-hour away from Chicago. The owners of this house were desperate to sell it, because although it was a nice, clean house, no one seemed to want to buy it, and because they had already signed a contract to buy another house.

Jane Garvey and her husband—real estate entrepeneurs in the Chicago area—decided to buy the house. Asking the seller what he needed, they discovered that he wanted $10,000 to make a down payment on the house he was going to buy, and that they would have to assume the existing first mortgage of approximately $35,000, making the total sales price about $45,000.

Working with a Partner

This was attractive to Jane because the house was worth $54,000.

"We got a partner to come up with the $10,000 down payment," says Jane. "So we were into it for nothing down. We gave the partner 50 percent of the deal.

198

"It cost us a grand total of $36 to rehab the house. It was in pretty good shape. Tenants had already been lined up to rent the home for $600 a month. They moved in within a week of the purchase. The payments on the $35,000 mortgage, including taxes and insurance, were close to $465 per month, so we were making a positive monthly cash flow of about $135, minus any maintenance costs, which were fairly minimal."

A new expressway has been constructed that gives Jane's rental home improved access. Partly because of this, and partly because of a good rental history and natural appreciation, the value of the home has taken a large jump and is now worth about $72,000.

The same tenants that moved into the house shortly after Jane and her partner bought still rent it. The monthly rent has climbed to $700, which increases the monthly cash flow significantly. The only complaint she has is one that other landlords would love to have: that her tenants are "a little too clean. They scrub things so hard," she remarks, "that they scrub the markings right off the dials on the stove.

Best Profit-to-Effort Ratio

It's a simple little deal, Jane admits. It takes very little of her time to manage. There are no hassles. She and her partner split a monthly cash flow of close to $200. Their equity in the appreciated property is approximately $37,000 and rising—an equity of which Jane is half owner. She and her partner plan to keep the home for a long time.

Although Jane has pulled off other real estate deals that have made more money, she thinks of this as her best deal because of the excellent profit-to-effort ratio she achieved with it. It was and is simplicity itself.

"Really, anybody could have done it," she concludes.

CHAPTER 45

Just a Little Bread and Butter

In 1984, an older "bread-and-butter" property caught the eye of Los Angeles real estate investor Art Stein. (The "bread-and-butter" designation means that it was a blue-collar property that was not necessarily attractive, but was nevertheless a solid income producer.) The downtown Los Angeles building housed eight retail units on the ground floor and ten apartments on the second floor.

Art wanted to buy the property, but was suffering from a malady common to entrepreneurs: he was cash-poor and couldn't make the down payment. So he brought in a partner—an attorney friend. (Doesn't everyone have an "attorney friend"?)

A Fanastic Deal

"I have an incredible deal here," Art told his prospective partner. "There's a building that the owner wants to sell for $150,000. It's free and clear. It needs some work to clean it up and get the right kind of tenants in. The owner wants 20 percent down, and will carry all the financing for 17 years at 10 percent interest. The building, just the way it is, is worth $300,000."

The seller-carried, $120,000 first mortgage would be a 17-year, 10 percent interest contract with payments as follows: for the first two years, there would be interest-only payments of $1,000 per month. After that, the monthly principal and interest payments would rise to $1,114 each month.

The owner had inherited the building from his father, and didn't know what its value was. He didn't want to keep it because it wasn't a beautiful, attractive property, and because he didn't know how to manage it. For example, he was renting the units for $100 a month, whereas comparable units were renting for $250 a month.

The deal seemed so perfect that Art's attorney friend was somewhat skeptical. Nevertheless, he decided to accept Art's offer to become a 50 percent partner in the deal in exchange for the cash necessary to get into it: $30,000 for the down payment plus a few miscellaneous costs.

The deal closed, and Art—the "sweat partner"—went to work cleaning up the property, making cosmetic improvements, and changing the tenants.

He also got the rents up to where they should have been all along. When he bought the property, it was generating $1,800 a month in rents. Within six months, the rents were up to $4,500 per month, and the positive cash flow, after expenses, was about $4,000.

In '87—about three years later—Art put additional financing on the property of $250,000 in the form of a new five-year second mortgage loan ($2,917 monthly payments).

He used $100,000 of the $250,000 loan to improve the building; split $70,000 cash in his and his partner's pockets; and used the remaining $80,000 to purchase a 24-unit rental property.

Making Some Dough

Today, the bread-and-butter property in downtown Los Angeles is producing a lot of bread for Art and his partner. Even with the $250,000 additional mortgage, it is generating a *positive cash flow of approximately $2,000 per month. Its current market value? A third of a million dollars!*

It must also be understood that this property produced the money to purchase the 24-unit property, which is currently generating a $3,000-a-month positive cash flow. So in a very real sense, Art's original no-down deal (no-down because he found a partner to come up with the cash for a down payment) has resulted in a half-share of $5,000 in positive monthly cash flow, plus very handsome equity positions in two solid pieces of real estate.

All of this did not come without a price, however—a price beyond the invested dollars and cents. It took work and management savvy. Art admits, "These buildings are management intensive. You really have to stay on top of them. I can't say they're easy to manage. If they were, everyone would be doing it. It takes some work." What Art doesn't mention is that it takes a certain amount of knowledge and experience to do it right—commodities he apparently has plenty of.

In Retirement

In the not too distant future, Art plans to refinance his bread-and-butter property by taking a new first mortgage out against it to pay off the existing first and second mortgages. "When we do, we'll put some more cash in our pockets," he laughs. Their equity position is such that they should easily be able to do that and still maintain a healthy positive cash flow.

"By the way, my partner and I have done this sort of thing many times in the last several years," Art points out. "He has made so much money on these deals that he's been able to retire from his law practice.

"That's real estate!"

CHAPTER 46

Easy Does It!

" I ran across a gentleman one day who told me he had a list of all the names of out-of-town property owners on computer," says Ron LeGrand, real estate investor and educator from Jacksonville, Florida. "He said I could pull out names based on whatever criteria I wanted."

Ron had him pull up all the names of out-of-town owners of single-family homes in the Jacksonville area that fell within a certain range of assessed value. He received a list of 4,445 names. This was early in 1991.

"I then wrote a one-page letter," Ron continues, "and sent it out to 500 of those names to see what would happen. It was a simple letter that basically said 'I buy houses in your area, and I noticed that you were from out of town. Would you be interested in selling?' I put a little reply card on the bottom for them to fill out the information and send it back."

Ron was thinking, of course, that out-of-town property owners, as a group, would be more motivated to sell than local owners.

Successful Communications

His letters were a success. Out of the 500 letters he sent, he got ten replies, and out of the ten replies, he ended up buying three houses.

Says Ron: "One owner wrote back and said she wanted $8,000 for her house. Upon further investigation, we discovered that she had not even seen the house in 22 years! She had it in the hands of a local management company, who had a tenant in it that was paying only $150 a month in a market where $400 had been the normal rent for many years."

The house was a concrete block building with a new roof and was in fairly good condition. Ron knew right off the bat that the property was worth $35,000, which was the low end of the market. Ron interviewed the tenant, and found that she had been living there for a long time and would love to own the house.

"To make a long story short," states Ron, "we accepted the owner's offer immediately, without arguing with her; we sent her a contract and asked her to sign it and send it back; we took it to the title company which sent around a deed to be signed with instructions; and we delivered the money.

"In order to deliver the money, I went out and got a first mortgage loan from a private lender for $17,000 (the lady owned the house free and clear). The lender didn't even ask for an appraisal. He just went out and looked at it. The terms of the loan were 18 percent interest, seven years, and $350-a-month payments.

Why a private lender with a high interest rate? "I didn't want to be personally liable for the loan," Ron explains. "It was a corporate loan, and I borrowed it as a corporate officer. Also, I didn't want to have to qualify to anybody. I didn't want it on my credit report. I've designed my life so that I don't have to qualify to anybody for anything. That's one of the things I teach in my real estate classes.

A Quick Turn

"After paying $8,000 for the house and over $1,500 for closing costs—which were high because it was a private loan and I went through a mortgage broker—I had about $7,500 left at closing. At that point I went to visit the tenant and said, 'Mary Ellen, would you like to own this house?' And she said 'Mr. LeGrand, I don't have any money to put down on it.' So I said, 'What if you not only didn't need any money to put down on it, but what I did these little repairs, that need to be done? Would you like to own the house then?' "

To which Mary Ellen replied, "Mr. Legrand, I would *love* to own this home! I think God sent you!"

Ron then explained that the rent she had been paying for years was way below what it should have been. She admitted that this was true. So Ron made the following deal with her: He immediately raised the rent to $350 per month, which she could afford, and told her that if she paid him $350 a month on time for a year, he would sell her the house for $35,000 with no down payment, and he would work out the terms of the 30-year mortgage loan so that she would continue paying $350 a month in mortgage payments for the entire term of the loan.

"What I did here," explains Ron, "was create a mortgage on which I was making $350 monthly payment for seven years, and then turn around and create another mortgage on which I would be getting $350 a month for 30 years, beginning *after* the year of $350-a-month rental payments."

The cash flow was structured to be a wash during the early years when Ron would be making loan payments on the seven-year note. But it is obvious that after he has paid off that mortgage, *he will continue to receive $350 each month for 24 years thereafter from the lady to whom he sold the property. That's a total of $100,800!*

The only loose end was the fact that Mary Ellen was 68 years old when he made the deal with her. He tied up this loose end by having her buy a mortgage life insurance policy with him as the beneficiary. This policy will pay him the balance of the $35,000 if she passes away before paying off the mortgage note, which is a strong possibility.

Realizing the American Dream

It should be noted that Ron could have dislodged this elderly lady from the rental home, done a little work on it, retailed it for $35,000 cash with an FHA or VA buyer, and walked away with a lot of cash almost immediately. Why didn't he do it? In his own words: "This lady deserved to live in that house. She had been there a long time. So I chose to leave her there. Instead of booting her out and doing the work, I decided to do what I did. The way it worked out, I got a pay day up front, and I'll get a pay day in the future.

"While this was a good money-maker, it certainly wasn't my most profitable deal," Ron points out. "But I think of it as my best deal because it was so simple and easy."

And, it might be added, it helped an elderly tenant finally realize the American Dreram of home ownership. That has to have something to do with it.

CHAPTER 47

The Flea-Trap That
Became a Treasure Chest

E d Shumaker surprised a lot of people when he bought what was considered to be one of Waukegan, Illinois' foremost "flea traps." After all, he was of sound mind, and even had a reputation for being a smart, level-headed investor.

So why did he purchase the 100-year-old, eight-unit apartment building that looked like it had been a test case for deferred maintenance since the late 1800s?

Looking Further Down the Road

The answer is simple. Ed was looking at the property's potential—not its current condition.

The building had been a big single-family home before World War II. But because of its close proximity to Great Lakes Naval Base in North Chicago, someone had done the patriotic thing during that war and converted the old home into apartments.

"I dealt directly with the owner," recalls Ed. "He was an attorney who had inherited the property, and wanted to get rid of it. It was in bad shape. But it had all the right things wrong with it."

The asking price was $23,500. Ed went to the local bank and told the president that he had located an eight-unit building for approximately $24,000, and would need another $8,000 for refurbishing.

The bank president said he would make a loan of only $24,000 (he didn't go for the extra $8,000 for refurbishing). And there would be one stipulation: $8,000 of the $24,000 loan would be withheld and released as the work was done—$4,000 upon completion of half the work, and the other $4,000 when all was finished.

Ed would make payments of $185.24 per month for the $24,000 loan. The interest rate was 8 percent and the term was 25 years.

Getting Creative

That was all well and fine, except that Ed needed more than the $16,000 the bank was going to give him up front. Sixteen thousand dollars was $7,500 short of what he needed just to purchase the house, and that didn't include a penny for improvements.

"So I went to the seller," he explains, "and offered him $17,500 cash—$16,000 from the bank loan and $1,500 from my pocket—if he would take back a second mortgage for $6,000 at 5 percent interest. He agreed, but wanted more interest. We settled on a 6½ percent rate, with monthly payments of $80 until the loan would be paid off in September of '79."

Ed came to the closing with the $23,500 sales price ($1,500 of his own money and $16,000 from the bank loan). After closing costs and all the prorations were tallied in, he got some money back, which meant that he actually only had to come up with about $1,000 dollars from his own pocket.

In short, Ed had paid close to $1,000 to purchase an eight-unit property. He had also stacked up two mortgages against that property for a total debt of $30,000, for which the combined monthly payments would be $265.24 for the first seven years, and then drop to $185.24 for 18 years after that. This borrowed money included $8,000 that he would draw as he made improvements.

Bang for His Bucks

By doing the refurbishing himself (with the help of a young man he hired for the job), Ed was able to get more bang for the $8,000 bucks set aside for improvements. In fact, he was able to do everything for approximately $7,500, and have about $500 enough left over to pay himself back half of the $1,000 he had taken out of his pocket to cover the balance of the purchase price.

This meant that he had only $500 of his own money into the deal.

The full refurbishing job took about a year, and included management improvements as well—especially when it came to the renters. For example, the tenants who were living on the third floor were parking their two cars and a pickup truck on the lawn because there was no parking for them. Ed solved this situation by dividing the apartment into two smaller units, moving an elderly man into one and an elderly woman into the other—neither of whom had cars. "So I increased the income on that floor," he says, "and solved the parking problem at the same time."

The property was suffering from a high vacancy rate when Ed took over. By applying correct property management principles, he solved this problem, too. "It didn't take me long to get it rented up," he claims.

The apartments' rents ranged from $90 to $205 a month at the time Ed assumed ownership. The rental income for the occupied units was averaging $681. One of his first goals was to get the rents up.

He did this by improving the units and the property in general, by carving out an additional rental unit, and by putting compact kitchens in each of the four small units on the second floor.

A property analysis sheet dated March 30, 1973 shows that Ed's efforts were fruitful. Within less than a year's time, he had pushed the monthly rental income up to a total of $1,125. That represents more than a 65 percent annual increase!

Operating expenses at that time averaged $223 per month. After those costs were deducted from the gross rents, and the $185.24 and $80 mortgage payments were made, Ed had a *monthly positive cash flow of $637*. This figure rose as time went by.

Ed had forced the value of the property up to about $65,000 with the physical improvements and his management efforts. Counting the $23,500 sales price and the $7,500 he invested in improvements, it is clear that Ed more than doubled the property's market value in less than a year.

Keeping It in the Family

In 1977, after five years of positive cash flow, *Ed sold the 9-unit property to his son, Mark, for $75,000,* with no down payment. The old home's rent-generating capacity by then had increased to the point that even after servicing the full $75,000 debt and paying operating expenses, Mark was making a $400-a-month positive cash flow. The property is worth approximately $150,000 today.

Some things are best kept in the family.

CHAPTER 48

The Right Way To Get Started

In 1983, Paul Shumaker bought a 22-unit building—one unit for each of his 22 years of age.

The son of Waukegan, Illinois real estate investor Ed Shumaker (also featured in this book), Paul had already launched his career in income-property investments when he heard about a converted bank building in North Chicago that a local savings and loan had taken back and was trying to get off its REO list.

Working jointly with his wife, Debbie, and aided by the expertise of his father, Paul purchased the property in early December of '83 for $160,000—only $7,272 per unit. At the time of the purchase, there were two small commercial units in the building, plus 20 residential apartments. It was originally a bank with apartments on the third floor, but had earlier been converted to all apartments except for two small commercial spaces.

Paul and Debbie came up with a $10,000 down payment, which they got from private sources. The balance of $150,000 was put on a 15-year, 8 percent interest mortgage note, with no payments for the first six months. (Because of Paul's youth, his father Ed had to co-sign the loan.) The 15 years of $1,433.48 monthly payments would begin after the six-month no-payment period.

Straightening Up the Situation

Although a professionl management company had been handling the building, only five of the units were occupied when Paul and Debbie assumed ownership, and some of those tenants didn't pay their rents. (This was a prime reason the savings and loan gave them six months before they had to start making payments.) One tenant moved out during the first week of their ownership.

If the vacancy situation was bad, the building itself was worse. "It was horrible," recalls Paul. "For example, when one of the tenants didn't pay his rent, the previous owner decided to take all the doors and windows off his apartment. The tenant happened to be a member of a motorcycle gang, so the whole gang rode their motorcycles through the hallways. It was this type of building when we bought it—bad!"

Bad as it was, Paul and Debbie rose to the challenge. They jumped into the thick of the battle, started cleaning, decorating, finding tenants, and generally whipping the physical building and its management into shape. They worked long hours. They even moved someone in on Christmas day.

Their efforts paid off. Within two months they had hacked the vacancy rate down to zero percent. Though they put in thousands of dollars worth of "sweat equity," their hard dollar costs during this initial period were minimal. (In the coming years, they would spend about $30,000 on improvements and giving the property a complete cosmetic overhaul. This money came from cash flow and personal sources.)

Maximizing Value

Paul soon began work to maximize the value of the square footage of the building by adding rentable units. "For instance," he says, "one of the units was quite large, and we had a difficult time keeping it rented. So we split it into an apartment and a small office space that were much easier to rent."

By the time he was finished, there were 26 units in all—two office spaces and 24 residential apartments. He also installed a new laundry room, complete with folding tables and new washers and dryers.

With the units all rented up, and a solid improvement program under way, Paul saw a dramatic change in the property's financial status. Gross rents shot up to an average of $5,855 per month. After deducting operating expenses and debt service costs, the young couple were realizing an approximate $20,000 annual positive cash flow.

A Shadow of Profits

That was good, but only a shadow of what it would eventually be. Today, thanks to an excellent management program, the 26 units and the laundry room produce a gross annual rent of over $131,000—close to $11,000 a month! Deducting all operating and debt service costs, *the annual positive cash flow produced by this real estate gem is about $60,000 or $5,000 a month.*

Moreover, *the property is now worth $725,000—$565,000 more than they paid for it not quite eight years ago.* In less than eight more years, the mortgage will be paid off and the property will be free and clear, unless Paul decides to sell, refinance, or work out a tax-deferred exchange before that time to put the huge dead equity to work.

A deal like this is sweet for an investor of any age. But youth has its advantages: the younger you are, the longer you're likely to enjoy the taste. Paul, who pulled off this deal at the tender age of 22, will enjoy its rewards with Debbie and their children for the rest of his life.

May it be a long one!

CHAPTER 49

The High-Stakes Hock

A money broker walked into Barney Zick's posh Kansas City office in 1974 and asked him to find $3 million for one of his clients. Although Barney was a successful business person and real estate entrepreneur, and had earned a reputation as a problem-solver, he was flattered that this man thought he could get that kind of funding.

"The broker's client had a 200-acre piece of ground on which he had started to build subdivisions," explains Barney. "But it was on the outside edge of town, which made it not all that popular. The developr had already put about $1 million of his own money into the development when the savings and loan that had made a commitment to him for a loan decided not to honor that commitment. So he was desperate to get funding."

Buying Some Time

Barney told the broker to contact his client and come back with a smaller sum—enough to buy time and keep him alive. He explained that he would have a better chance of coming up with $300,000 or half a millon, and could definitely raise $50,000 or $100,000 to keep things going until the rest of the money could be raised.

Barney also told the broker that he bought and sold mortgages, and that if the client had any mortgages, he might be willing to buy them at a discount.

The broker came back with a list of what he claimed was $800,000 worth of property. However, $500,000 of it was comprised of municipal debentures that were to be paid basically whenever the city wanted to pay. Barney was not interested in these.

"I came up with about $300,000 worth of hard equities—mortgage notes and properties, including raw land," says Barney, "and said that I would buy them for $150,000 cash. Actually, about $200,000 of the $300,000 consisted of mortgages. I said I would buy them within a corporation, and give the developer an option to buy the stock back for $180,000 at the end of a year's time. The advantage for him would be that he'd get the cash, and the notes and properties would be off his books in case he got into financial trouble. He'd have an option on them, but an option is not something that a creditor would want to go after.

"I also stipulated that I would have the right to the income generated by the assets in the portfolio until the option was exercised, plus the right to buy and sell properties within the corporation (with the safeguard that I would first get the approval of the bank), and the right to clean up the portfolio. I could see problems with some of the properties in it."

Around Robin Hood's Bank

Barney didn't hear from anyone about his offer for two full months, which was surprising given the fact that the money broker's client was desperate to get the funds. He found out later that the broker thought that Barney's offer was so unusual and promising that he decided to try to do the same thing himself, and consequently attempted to go around him, spending two months going from bank to bank to raise the money to pull it off.

He didn't succeed, and when the developer found out what was going on, he called Barney directly and said he wanted to go ahead with the deal. But he would need the money within a week. This struck Barney as a real problem, since his glimpse of the assets he would be getting told him that it would take at least 30 days to clean up the problems that existed with them.

There was also the *small* matter of getting the $150,000 within a week. Barney had previously broached the subject of this particular deal with his banker, who thought it sounded attractive, at least in theory. Now that the deal was on, with a screaming time restriction, he rushed to his banker and asked to borrow $150,000 against the $300,000 worth of assets, which mostly consisted of second mortgages.

The banker said it looked like a good deal, exept that it was the bank's policy not to make loans against second mortgages. Barney then asked if he would make a loan against corporate stock.

The banker said, "Yes, we can do that. What stock do you have? IBM? General Motors?"

"It's a lot smaller company than that," said Barney. "Its assets will be about $300,000. But I only want to borrow $150,000 and I will give you all the stock in the corporation as collateral."

"That's what we call a closely-held corporation," said the banker.

"That's right," replied Barney. "But as additional collateral, I've got about $300,000 of assets I'll pledge."

The banker said Barney had the go-ahead as long as the loan was made against corporate stock, rather than second mortgages, and as long as all the problems with the notes and properties within the portfolio were cleared up.

Creative Thinking

With that, Barney rushed over to his lawyer's office and formed a new corporation called First Mortgage Company of Kansas City, Inc. The bank then approved the $150,000 loan against the corporate stock, plus additional collateral, contingent upon clearing up the problems. The loan would be good for thirteen months, since the developer could buy back the property at the end of twelve months.

Recalls Barney: "I still had to solve the problem of having to fix up the problems and close in seven days. The idea I came up with, and the banker agreed to, was that the banker would write out a sight draft for $150,000 that said that when presented to the bank with the specified legal documents and confirmation that the problems had been solved, the $150,000 loan would be dispersed.

"So we outlined the 20 or more notes and properties and specified 30 things that had to be taken care of. For instance, the developer had to resolve a *right to renew* clause on a note that was supposed to have been paid the previous year. The developer had told me that the right to renew was only good for one year, but I said I needed to see something in writing. As it turned out, it was good for three years.

"Anyway, I handed the developer the sight draft for $150,000, and he asked if he could go cash it right then. I said, 'You can cash it as soon as you do these things on the list.' That way, he had to do a lot of work, which was important because of the time element."

As it turned out, the developer took three months to do everything on the list. But by showing his creditors the sight draft for $150,000, he was able to keep everyone at bay. When all was complete, he got the $150,000. This gave him new life. However, at the end of the one-year option period, he didn't have the money to exercise it and get his $300,000 worth of mortgages and properties back.

"He called and said he was going to sue me," says Barney. "He had some loose reasons that were very vague. I said, 'Are you just trying to tell me that you want to buy another 30 days?' He admitted that he was.

"So I said, 'Look, we're big boys, and a game is a game. However, I will give you another 30 days. Let's not tie up any more legal fees.'

"By the end of the 30 days, he still hadn't been able to come up with the money, so I went over and helped him load up the few belongings that he had left, and he took off for another town. He had been living in a beautiful, 7,000 square foot home, but had been forced to move into a small, modest townhouse."

The developer may have been down, but not out. "Four years later I flew into the college town where I got my undergraduate degree," laughs Barney "and a guy pulled up in a red Cadillac convertible. It was the same developer. He was talking on a car phone, and a secretary sitting next to him was holding a second phone for him that was on hold. 'Hey Barney!' he shouted, 'Come on by the house. I've got a 7,000 square foot home on seven acres outside of town!' He was the typical wheeler-dealer type that had his ups and downs."

An Improved Portfolio

What about Barney? He used the corporation he had created for this deal and the $300,000 worth of assets he had purchased for half price as the solid base from which he expanded his mortgage and income property business.

During the year option period, Barney was active in managing the portfolio. In his own words: "It was a lot of fun. During that year I exchanged some of the properties; I rented some of the properties; I sold some of the properties. I overhauled the portfolio. At the end of the year's time, half the properties had changed, and the net worth of the portfolio had gone from $300,000 to $500,000. So the portfolio the developer walked away from at the end of the option period was much bigger than the portfolio he gave me at the beginning."

For those who know Barney, that should come as no surprise.

CHAPTER 50

The 1,500-Mile Deal

R eal estate is not generally considered to be a portable investment. But Dick Hamilton's best real estate deal was born in Indianapolis and traveled over 1,500 miles to Salt Lake City where it blossomed into maturity.

In 1985 a real estate agent Dick knew called and said he wanted to show him a prestigious, seven-story apartment building in an excellent residential area of Indianapolis.

"I can't afford a property like that," exclaimed Dick.

"I know you can't afford it," said the agent, "but I want to see it and the only way I can do that is to show it to a prospective buyer."

Love at First Sight

Dick agreed as a favor. Almost reluctantly, he went with the agent to see the property. That was all it took. It was love at first sight. The beautiful, older property had leaded glass windows, a walnut entry area, and a classic elevator with a picturesque brass gate. Figuring that the market value would have been well over $500,000 at the time, Dick decided to try to buy it.

"When I want to buy a piece of real estate," he explains, "I always try to get to know what the seller wants to accomplish with the sale. In this case, I discovered that the seller needed cash badly to do another real estate development. He had received some offers for the property, but they were all with $50,000 or $100,000 down payments, and he needed cash.

"So I made him an offer and although he wanted about $500,000, he took it. It was an offer for $325,000. There would be a $250,000 cash down payment—that was what made it work—and the seller would carry the balance of $75,000 on a second mortgage. The seller was reluctant to accept the $325,000 total sales price, but he needed cash, and a quarter of a million dollars cash was hard for him to pass up right then."

Dick went to the bank and told his banker that he had found the bargain of a lifetime: he could buy a building worth over $500,000 for $325,000. The only problem, he explained, was that he needed $250,000 for a down payment.

The banker, with whom Dick had already established a successful track record, agreed, as long as the property's appraisal came in high enough to support the loan (which it did).

Best of Both Worlds

He agreed so readily that Dick asked for an extra $10,000, and got a loan for $260,000. "I literally put $10,000 in my pocket," states Dick. "The seller got his $250,000 in cash, and took back the $75,000 note."

Dick also got the building, of course, which performed financially as beautifully as it looked. It immediately gave him a $15,000 annual positive cash flow, and was relatively easy to manage.

Because interest rates were quite high when Dick incurred the $260,000 and $75,000 mortgages on the apartment building, he refinanced for approximately $400,000 about a year later with a 20-year loan, having a 10-year call. "This was one of those unusual cases where you have the best of both worlds," he recalls. "When I refinanced, I not only lowered my payments, but I shortened the term of the loan, *and still put $65,000 into my pocket.*"

At this point in the game, Dick had taken a total of $75,000 cash out of the property, plus approximately $15,000 in positive cash flow. What had he put into it? Other than guts, brains, and experience, nothing.

Taking His Deal on the Road

A year and a half later, Dick took his deal on the road, so to speak. He moved to Salt Lake City, and shortly thereafter received an offer to buy his Indianapolis apartment building for $627,000 cash!

Attached as he was to the prestige apartment property, it was an offer Dick couldn't refuse. Due to a $20,000 problem that arose with a mechanical system within the building that had to be rectified, the actual net sales price turned out to be $607,000 cash.

With this substantial sum, Dick paid off the existing mortgage balance, which was still close to $400,000. This left him with a little more than $200,000 cash, out of which he had to pay over $20,000 worth of fees, commissions, and other closing costs.

When all was paid and done, *Dick walked away from the closing with approximately $180,000 in cash.*

He hadn't walked very far, however, before he realized that this would not look good on his tax return.

The smart thing to do in such a situation is to scramble to pull off a 1031 exchange and defer the tax consequences. So Dick scrambled and found two medical buildings in the south part of the Salt Lake Valley. One building had 29,000 square feet of space, the other 24,000 square feet.

"They were owned by the same people, but had both been repossessed by two different banks," Dick explains. "The smaller of the two buildings had a pharmacy and several doctors in it. It was fairly full and cash was flowing. So I paid more for that one than for the bigger one: $740,000."

The down payment was set for $74,000, with the $666,000 balance placed on a 25-year, 10¼ percent interest mortgage held by the bank that had repossessed it.

"I bought the other larger building," Dick continues, "which was behind the other one, for a little less: $730,000. The bank that owned it gave me a super deal because they really wanted to get rid of it, and were willing to make me a good deal if I closed before the end of the year and got it off their books."

He paid 10 percent cash down for this building—$73,000, and the bank that was selling it carried the $657,000 balance on a 10-year mortgage. The mortgage payments were set up on a graduated, adjustable schedule.

Breathing Easy

Where did the $73,000 and $74,000 cash down payments come from? As the perceptive reader will already have surmised, they came from the $180,000 cash Dick walked away with from the sale of his Indiana apartment building, using the 1031 exchange. After making the $147,000 total cash down payments on the two medical buildings, Dick had about $33,000 left, which he plowed into his new properties in the form of miscellaneous costs and improvements.

All of this made his tax accountant breath easier, and for Dick, the tax-deferred exchange was easier than expected. 'It's really not that complicated—especially after you've done one," he claims. "There are certain hoops you have to jump through and requirements you have to meet, but it's really not painful."

Although the two medical buildings have generated a slight negative cash flow until recently, and are only now beginning to break even, a positive cash flow in the future looks like a sure thing, especially now that the local economy is picking up.

Dick is proud of his two properties, which he manages himself. "In fact," he remarks. "I just got a call from one of my biggest tenants. They've got a circuit breaker problem. So I'll be down there in a few minutes checking out the circuit breakers."

Thank Heavens for Real Estate

When he reflects on the deal that started with an apartment building in Indianapolis, and which came of age with over 1½ million dollars worth of medical buildings in Salt Lake City, Dick blesses the day he decided to invest in real estate.

In his own words: "Now I own these two beautiful properties, which I never would have dreamed of owning when I first got into this business in 1980. And they were made possible by a deal clear across the country on another property that I never would have imagined owning—a deal that put $75,000 in my pocket plus a lot of cash flow even before I sold it.

"When I think about it, I realize it's nothing short of amazing!"